THE POCKET IDIOT'S GUIDE™ TO

Direct Stock Investing

Douglas Gerlach and Lita Epstein

ALPHA

A member of Penguin Group (USA) Inc.

ALPHA BOOKS

Published by the Penguin Group

Penguin Group (USA) Inc., 375 Hudson Street, New York, New York 10014, USA

Penguin Group (Canada), 90 Eglinton Avenue East, Suite 700, Toronto, Ontario M4P 2Y3, Canada (a division of Pearson Penguin Canada Inc.)

Penguin Books Ltd., 80 Strand, London WC2R 0RL, England

Penguin Ireland, 25 St. Stephen's Green, Dublin 2, Ireland (a division of Penguin Books Ltd.)

Penguin Group (Australia), 250 Camberwell Road, Camberwell, Victoria 3124, Australia (a division of Pearson Australia Group Pty. Ltd.)

Penguin Books India Pvt. Ltd., 11 Community Centre, Panchsheel Park, New Delhi—110 017, India

Penguin Group (NZ), 67 Apollo Drive, Rosedale, North Shore, Auckland 1311, New Zealand (a division of Pearson New Zealand Ltd.)

Penguin Books (South Africa) (Pty.) Ltd., 24 Sturdee Avenue, Rosebank, Johannesburg 2196, South Africa

Penguin Books Ltd., Registered Offices: 80 Strand, London WC2R 0RL, England

THE POCKET IDIOT'S GUIDE TO and Design are trademarks of Penguin Group (USA) Inc.

International Standard Book Number: 978-1-59257-995-2
Library of Congress Catalog Card Number: 2009934675

12   11   10   8   7   6   5   4   3   2   1

Interpretation of the printing code: The rightmost number of the first series of numbers is the year of the book's printing; the rightmost number of the second series of numbers is the number of the book's printing. For example, a printing code of 10-1 shows that the first printing occurred in 2010.

Printed in the United States of America

Note: This publication contains the opinions and ideas of its authors. It is intended to provide helpful and informative material on the subject matter covered. It is sold with the understanding that the authors and publisher are not engaged in rendering professional services in the book. If the reader requires personal assistance or advice, a competent professional should be consulted.

The authors and publisher specifically disclaim any responsibility for any liability, loss, or risk, personal or otherwise, which is incurred as a consequence, directly or indirectly, of the use and application of any of the contents of this book.

Most Alpha books are available at special quantity discounts for bulk purchases for sales promotions, premiums, fund-raising, or educational use. Special books, or book excerpts, can also be created to fit specific needs.

For details, write: Special Markets, Alpha Books, 375 Hudson Street, New York, NY 10014.

Contents

Introduction

If you think you need thousands of dollars just to start building a stock portfolio, you're wrong. You can start with as little as $10 per week or per month using dividend reinvestment plans or DRIPs. You may need to invest a bit more to get started with direct stock purchases, or DSPs, but most companies allow you to make additional investments of $10 to $50 per investment.

So you don't have to be wealthy or pay an expensive broker to build your own portfolio of stocks. You can build a sizeable portfolio and never pay a commission to a stockbroker. Instead of paying commissions, that money can go directly into growing your portfolio.

We'll show you how to get started with the basics of DRIPs and DSPs and how to buy your first shares. Then we talk about how to research and pick companies. We explore how to set up an account and review the role of account administrators. Then we talk about basic direct stock investing strategies. We discuss some problems you need to avoid when using direct investing. And finally we discuss the tax implications and tax strategies for direct investors.

We've also developed some little helpers you'll find throughout the book:

def•i•ni•tion

You'll find meanings to words you might not understand.

Direct Aids

You'll find tips for how to improve your direct investing skills.

Purchase Pitfalls

You'll find warnings for things you should avoid as a direct investor.

Stock Facts

You'll find interesting information about direct investing.

Acknowledgements

We want to thank everyone at Penguin Books that made this book possible, especially Paul Dinas, who first contacted us about writing this book. We also want to thank our development editor, Phil Kitchel, for his outstanding job of editing and keeping this project together; and our copy editor, Sonja Nikkila, for watching all those details.

Chapter 1

Why Invest in Stocks Directly?

In This Chapter

- What are DRIPs and DSPs?
- Investing automatically
- Using IRAs
- Tax traps
- Dealing with investment fears

You might think stock investing is only the domain of people with lots of money to invest. Those big players include the wealthiest people, who can afford to hire expensive brokers to manage a portfolio of common stocks. You're not in that league, so you think stock investing is out of your reach.

Think again. We'll show you how—with as little as $10 to spare—you can begin to set aside money to buy shares of stock in companies like IBM, Sears Roebuck, Rubbermaid, Coca-Cola, AT&T, McDonald's, or Xerox. With persistence and patience, over time you can invest on a regular basis and build a sizeable portfolio. You'll never have to pay a stockbroker a commission, but you do have to watch out for fees, which we'll show you how to do.

In this chapter, we'll introduce you to the two major types of direct stock investing—DRIPs and DSPs.

What Is a DRIP?

A DRIP, which stands for dividend reinvestment plan, allows you to reinvest any dividends you earn from a company in buying more shares of that company—without paying any commissions for buying the new shares. Do be careful though, because some companies are charging for reinvesting dividends, so check your fees carefully.

Publicly traded companies run DRIP programs for their shareholders. Instead of sending dividend checks to shareholders enrolled in a company's DRIP, the company reinvests those dividends by purchasing additional shares (or fractional shares) in the shareholder's name.

In some cases, you only need to buy one share of a stock before you can enroll in a company's DRIP; other companies may require you to buy 10 or more shares. The company will then reinvest your dividends without a fee or commission, as long as you sign up for the company's DRIP. In fact, before even buying that first share, you should research a company's fee structure to be sure you won't be losing too much of your investment to fees. We talk more about how to do that in Chapter 2.

Over 1,600 companies have dividend reinvestment plans for their shareholders, and some companies have DRIPs that are enormously popular with their shareholders. RPM, a Fortune 500 specialty chemical company, reports that 71 percent of its shareholders are enrolled in its DRIP. Over 64 percent of the shareholders of AFLAC, a company that sells supplemental life insurance policies, are enrolled in that company's DRIP.

Companies like DRIPs for several reasons. DRIPs provide a stable base of shareholders who are likely to have a long-term "buy and hold" investment philosophy. Individuals, particularly those who use *dollar-cost averaging* to add shares to their DRIPs, may see the drop in a stock's share price as a buying opportunity, as opposed to institutions and traders who move rapidly in and out of stocks with short-term goals in mind. They will quickly run to get out of a stock on even a whisper of a bad quarterly report.

def•i•ni•tion

> **Dollar-cost averaging** is an investment strategy where you invest equal dollar amounts regularly and periodically over specific time periods (such as $100 monthly) in a particular investment or portfolio.

This base of individual shareholders who choose to stay with a company over the long haul can help stabilize a company's share price. DRIPs keep capital inside the company. Since the company does not have to pay cash dividends outright to DRIP participants, those reinvested dividends can help maintain cash flow via additional share purchases. DRIPs can also help companies to raise additional capital without making a public offering.

The best part of this deal is that, in most cases, you don't have to pay a commission, so you can get additional shares of stock through a DRIP with a purchase of as little as $10 or $25. Most companies offer you the opportunity to buy shares in addition to your dividend reinvestment, called optional cash purchases (OCPs). Many companies allow these OCPs on a regular schedule, usually once or twice a month or sometimes quarterly, but you do need to read the fine print because others charge for each cash investment.

When you make OCPs, the company purchases the shares for you. You will get a statement that details the shareholder's account, usually on a quarterly basis.

In Chapter 3, we explore the numerous ways you can buy your first share of stock and get started with building your own DRIP portfolio.

What Is a DSP?

Some companies do not require you to buy your first share from a stockbroker. You can actually start buying shares directly from the company. This type of plan is called a direct stock purchase (DSP) plan, and about 570 corporations offer this option today.

The big difference with DSPs is that you don't have to find a way to buy the first share before you can start buying stock directly with a company. Otherwise the plans work in a similar way to DRIPs. We talk more about how to get started with DSPs in Chapter 3.

Watch Out for Fees

You will find that most DRIPs and DSPs charge little or nothing to buy additional shares of stock. But you will find some have a fee structure that makes direct stock investment just as expensive, or more expensive, than working with an online discount broker. Higher and higher fees are popping up each day as some companies hire administrators that increase fees and make direct stock investing less attractive as a low-cost alternative. Sometimes these high fees ruin plans offered by great companies.

For example, suppose a plan caps its fees at $2.50. You may not think this sounds like much, but if you invest $25 a month, the fee would gobble up 10 percent of your investment. If you invest $250 a month, the $2.50 would mean 1 percent of your investment is going to fees. We explore the impact of fees more closely in Chapter 11, when we talk about the potential problems of direct stock investing.

Account Administrators

Many DSPs and DRIPs are not managed by the company. Instead the company hires an outside administrator, usually a bank, to handle all stock purchases and all optional cash purchases. We talk more about the role of account administrators in Chapter 6.

Following Your Statements

A big drawback of managing a portfolio with DSPs and DRIPs is that you'll be getting statements from each of the companies with whom you have an account. Since a well-balanced portfolio usually has 10 to 20 stocks, as your portfolio grows, so will your paperwork.

In Chapter 7, we'll talk more about how to read your statements and how to use portfolio management tools.

Automatic Investments

One of the biggest advantages of investing using direct stock investments is that you can set aside a specific amount per month or per quarter to gradually build a strong portfolio of stocks. This amount can be as little as $10 or $25 per month with some companies, but do watch out for fees.

If you do plan to invest less than $100 per purchase, be sure you are working with companies that do not charge fees with each automatic investment. We'll talk more about why automatic investing works as an investment strategy in Chapter 8.

IRAs and Direct Stock Investing

You can use direct stock investing as a tool to build your Individual Retirement Account (IRA), but you may need to use a third-party service to do so. We'll explore how to set up a direct investing IRA account in Chapter 9.

Synthetic DRIPs

You can now reinvest dividends through brokers that manage synthetic DRIPs. This type of DRIP is not a "real" DRIP, it's more of a service that the brokers provide to their customers and is often referred to as a "synthetic DRIP."

The big advantage of using a synthetic DRIP is that brokers will allow you to drip (make small, regular investments in a stock) many companies that do not even have a formal DRIP program. If your broker offers this feature, you can drip virtually every blue-chip company on the U.S. stock exchanges.

Although synthetic DRIPs give you the ability to expand the number of drippable companies, they do have a few drawbacks. The biggest drawback is that synthetic DRIPs do not allow for fractional share ownership—only full shares can be purchased and the remainder of the dividend is deposited as cash into your trading account. Real DRIPs do allow you to buy fractional shares.

The second drawback of brokerage-run DRIPs is that share purchase plans are not available. If you want to buy additional shares, you have to pay the regular commission price of your broker. We talk more about synthetic DRIPs in Chapter 10.

DRIPs, DSPs, and Taxes

Filing your taxes can be a nightmare when you use direct stock investing. You'll have difficulty calculating the value and yield of your investments. You will need to break down all dividend income, capital gains, and possible deductions from all of your DRIP investments.

Generally, you will only get two pieces of information from each company through which you've bought your DRIPs or DSPs to help you file taxes: account statements and a 1099-DIV.

At the end of the year, each DRIP or DSP will send you and the IRS a copy of the 1099-DIV form. This form reports all dividends and distributions paid to you over the past year. Dividends that are reinvested are considered a paid dividend at the time they are reinvested. So even though you reinvested the dividend you will need to pay taxes on it.

Each time a transaction occurs (dividend reinvestment, optional cash payment, stock split, and so on), the DRIP or DSP will provide you with an updated account statement for the year. Be sure to keep the last account statement for the year, as this is the only hard copy that you will receive showing your transactions. Start a file for each company and keep these statements. You'll need them to calculate long-term capital gains when you sell the stock.

We explore how to deal with taxes in greater detail in Chapter 12.

Getting Past Your Fears

You may think that creating and maintaining a stock portfolio is beyond your skill level and a task that is better left to professionals. But if you take the time to learn how to pick companies (which we talk about in Chapter 2), you can minimize investment risk and cut your investment costs by doing it yourself.

The process of picking stocks is not as difficult as some would have you believe. You may even find it fun. In fact if you don't find it fun, you might be better off using *no-load mutual funds* rather than trying to build your own stock portfolio. By picking mutual funds managed by professional stock managers, you don't have to worry about picking the best stocks.

If you do enjoy researching stocks and finding the best companies for your portfolio, then direct stock investing can be rewarding. Just remember that patience is the key to being a successful direct stock investor.

def•i•ni•tion

> A **no-load mutual fund** is a portfolio of stocks managed by a professional stock manager, but you don't have to pay an up-front commission to buy the mutual fund's shares.

As a DRIP investor, you must be willing to invest for the long term, taking the time to pick the right companies but continuing to monitor the success of those companies. While we don't suggest you buy a company and hold it forever, you must be willing to hold onto a company through the ups and downs of the stock market. You can't be someone who pushes the panic button and sells all their stocks as soon as there is some bad economic news.

Patient investors know that when a stock is down, as long as they believe in the company, that's the best time to buy more shares. But don't just continue to invest blindly. Do the research to find out why a stock is down and whether or not you truly do believe the company will recover from whatever sent its stock price falling. We'll be talking more about how to research companies in Chapter 2.

Regardless of your age, investing can trigger emotional reactions that lead to mistakes, so the most important trait that you will need as an investor is patience. Before you embark on building a good portfolio, then, it's necessary to remind yourself that doing so involves long-term thinking, not short-term wins.

Purchase Pitfalls

The biggest mistake any investor can make is to buy high and sell low. Don't panic and sell a stock just because its price dropped. Do your own research and determine whether or not you believe in the company's future before you think of selling.

Some people see no difference between day trading and investing. A day trader is someone who holds stocks for just one day and ends the day in a cash position. Some traders will hold stocks for a few days or even a few months. If that's the type of trader you are, then direct stock investing is not for you. You're much better off getting the best deal with a discount online broker.

As a direct stock investor, you must want to build a core portfolio for the long term. If you already own stocks and believe you've got the basics in place for a core portfolio, you can research your company holdings and see if they offer DRIPs or DSPs.

The best place to start your research will be to call the investor relations department and ask if the company offers a DRIP or DSP. If they do, ask them to send you plan information and the forms needed to start a DRIP or DSP account.

If you don't have a core portfolio, this is a great time to establish one. Start slowly and think about a good balance of stocks. Since you're looking at stocks that pay dividends, in most cases you will be looking for blue-chip companies. (Few technology firms pay dividends, and most that do have not set up DRIP or DSP programs.) These types of blue-chip stocks make a great core portfolio that you can use to build up a well-balanced nest egg. You can use this DRIP/DSP portfolio to accumulate assets while reducing risk using dollar-cost averaging.

If you follow the plan and invest regularly, you will find that you have built up substantial numbers of shares that ultimately will help you build great wealth.

So are you ready to get started? Let's explore how to pick the companies you want to add to your portfolio.

The Least You Need to Know

- DRIPs and DSPs allow you to invest with as little as $10 per month.
- When choosing companies you must be sure to watch out for fees.
- Taxes on DRIPs and DSPs can be complicated to calculate. Be sure you keep all your year-end statements.
- Patience is the key for DRIP/DSP investments. If you're the type of person who panics and sells all stocks if the market falls, this is probably not the type of investing for you.

Chapter 2

Choosing a Company

In This Chapter

- Seeking out companies
- Acting defensively
- Looking for quality
- Portfolio management

As you start looking for companies to include in your stock portfolio, whether through DSPs or DRIPs, your primary goal is to find companies that you'll want to own for a very long time—if not forever. Remember, you're beginning what hopefully will be a long-term relationship with the companies that you select.

In this chapter, we review the key factors you should consider when picking stocks for your portfolio. We also recommend websites where you can research your picks.

Finding Your Companies

Since you know you want to invest using direct stock investing plans, you automatically limit your choices to the approximately 1,600 companies that offer those plans. Companies do not usually give information on their websites because of strict government regulations, so you'll need to call the investor relations offices of the companies that you pick.

You may be wondering how you can possibly narrow down your choices from the thousands of companies that exist out there. Luckily, there are two good websites that narrow those choices for you. DripCentral (www.dripcentral.com) is managed by author Douglas Gerlach. He lists good choices in his online book about direct stock investing. When you get to the website, go to his online book, *DRIP Investing, Step by Step*. In Chapter 2, you'll see a page called "Buying a Single Share Direct from the Company." Click on that link and you'll find an excellent list of companies from which you can choose stocks for your portfolio. We highlight the top companies from that list in Appendix C.

Wall-Street.com (www.wall-street.com/directlist. html) focuses on about 700 companies that it believes have the most potential. The site has confined its list to those companies that the American Association of Individual Investors covers for its members.

These lists give you a good starting point, but you need to own your choices, so do your own research as well. One good place to start is to read articles about the most respected companies in magazines such as *Fortune* or *Forbes*. As you read those stories, see which of the companies that interest you are on

the list of companies that offer direct stock investing programs. When you narrow your list down
to about 10 companies, call the investor relations
office and ask them for information about their
direct stock investing plan. They could call it a
DRIP program or DSP plan.

Purchase Pitfalls

Remember, you want to find the companies you can stick with for a long
time, so do your research diligently. If you
don't, you could lose valuable time and the
opportunity for long-term investing growth.

Start Defensively

As you pick the stocks and industries you want to
focus on, think defensively. Look for industries
that survive during the good times and the bad.
Some top defensive industries to consider (in
alphabetical order) include:

- Consumer products
- Energy (can be cyclical, so expect more ups
  and downs)
- Finance
- Food and beverages
- Pharmaceuticals
- Utilities

Consumer Products

The companies that fall into this category are those that sell the little things we always need, such as shampoo, toothpaste, paper goods, shoes, and shirts—the kinds of items we buy in good times and bad. We group major retailers such as Wal-Mart and Home Depot on this list, as well as leading consumer product companies such as Clorox, Colgate-Palmolive, Gillette, and Kimberly-Clark. This category can also have overlaps with pharmaceuticals in companies such as Johnson & Johnson. You'll find others on the direct stock investing list in Appendix C.

Energy

Energy can be more cyclical than the rest of the industries we mention, but it also can have the greatest potential for long-term gains. Oil price fluctuations can be among the greatest challenges for energy companies. Government control and international cartels also make it difficult for energy companies to maintain their profits. But some good companies that have survived many storms include Exxon Mobil and Chevron Texaco. You'll find others on the direct stock investing lists we've recommended.

Finance

Financial services and banks can have good and bad years. In fact, as we've seen in 2008 and 2009, they can have *really* bad years, but that doesn't

mean they won't come back strong. Banks, like
food and consumer products, are needed in good
and bad times. Factors that can have an impact
on this industry include interest rates, investments, value of the dollar, and people's ability to
repay loans. But in most years banks pay regular
dividends and make good investment choices for
direct stock investing. Some good choices include
American Express, JPMorgan Chase, and Morgan
Stanley, but there are dozens of other smaller
banks to look at as well.

Food and Beverages

No matter what happens to the economy, people
have to eat and drink, so companies that sell
food and beverages can make excellent long-term
investment options. You can pick from some of the
best food and beverage companies that offer direct
stock investing, including Campbell Soup, Coca-
Cola, General Mills, Heinz, Hershey, Kellogg,
Philip Morris, PepsiCo, Sara Lee, and Tricon.
You'll find others on the direct stock investing lists
we've recommended.

Pharmaceuticals

Everyone, no matter what the state of the economy,
needs to fill prescriptions, so the pharmaceutical
industry does well in both good and bad times.
Many other factors also make the pharmaceutical
industry attractive over the long term.

- The Food and Drug Administration fast-track drug approval process enables drugs to get on the market faster and start making money for the company.

- An aging world population needs more drugs to treat more illnesses as they get older.

- Patent protection gives a company exclusive rights to sell a drug.

Not all of the pharmaceutical companies have direct stock investing plans, but many of them do. Two excellent ones include Johnson & Johnson and Pfizer. You'll find others on the direct stock investing lists we've recommended.

This list by no means includes all the industries you might want to consider. Almost every industry group has one or two good choices. For example, in the entertainment industry, one company that has shown it can ride out any storm is The Walt Disney Company. General Electric (GE), the world's biggest conglomerate, is another company to consider. GE is heavily invested in alternative energy and medical technology. In the construction industry, you may want to look at Caterpillar and John Deere.

Qualities You Should Seek

How do you know if you've picked a good company? The first thing you should do is go to the company's website and download the last three to five years of annual reports. You can find those annual reports in the investor relations section of the company's website.

Any industry that you do decide to consider should have these key factors:

- Visibility and long-term opportunity
- Strong growth potential and a strong history of growth, year after year
- Predictable earnings—a solid earnings stream over at least 5 to 10 years

It should also be a company you understand—don't invest in a company whose products or services are foreign to you. In order to determine whether or not a company is continuing to do well, you must understand its products and growth potential.

Direct Aids

If you prefer to get copies of the original annual reports, you can call the investor relations department and ask for copies or you can request copies by mail on the company's website.

Following is a checklist of some of the qualities you should seek.

Most Respected Company in the Industry

As you research company options, look for companies that are listed among the most respected in the industry. *Fortune* and *Forbes* magazines are good places to start, but you can also research associations within the industry to find the most respected companies.

Profitable Business

If you've done speculative investing in the past, you may have been willing to buy a growth stock that was not yet making any money. That's a big no-no when you're picking a stock for long-term investing through a direct stock investing plan.

Be sure the companies you pick have a long history of earning profits. You can find this out by reviewing the company's annual reports, as well as by using key financial websites, such as Yahoo! Finance (http://finance.yahoo.com).

When you search for a company at Yahoo! Finance, on the first page you will see two key statistics to check: "EPS" (earnings per share) and "Div & Yield" (dividend and yield).

If the company isn't earning anything per share, it likely isn't paying dividends. Some companies will continue to pay dividends even in a bad year, but that won't go on for long. Don't even think about a company that doesn't have a positive number in earnings per share. If you like the company, you can put it on a watch list for the future, but don't start a long-term relationship with a company that currently has a negative earnings-per-share number.

"Div & Yield" will give you two numbers. The first is the yearly dividend that is paid and the second represents the yield, or the percentage the dividend earns based on the amount you pay for the stock. For example, if you pay $100 for a stock that pays a $2 dividend, the yield would be 2 percent. The stock's EPS should be higher than the dividend, or it's a likely sign that the company will not be able to continue to pay that level of dividend.

Purchase Pitfalls

If you find during your research that no dividend is paid, then cross that stock off your list. Even if a direct stock investing plan is offered by the company, there won't be any dividends to reinvest, which makes this option inferior to stocks that do pay dividends.

Cash on Hand

You should always check a company's cash position before buying a stock. If a company has little cash and lots of debt, you don't want to consider that company.

You can find out a company's cash on hand by searching for the company at Yahoo! Finance. On the left side of the company's summary page you'll see a list of links. Click on "Key Statistics" and go down the list to "Balance Sheet." There you will find the total cash the company has on hand, as well as its cash per share. You'll also find the company's total debt.

Another helpful statistic in that section is the current ratio. If the number is less than 1, that means the company may have trouble paying its bills. You should only consider companies with a current ratio over 1.

Increasing Dividends

As you look through the financial reports of a company, review its history of dividend payments. Your best bet is to pick companies that have continually raised dividends over the years.

If a company's dividend goes up and down, that's not a good sign. You won't be able to count on that company for the long term in your DRIP, so pick another in the same industry with a better history of paying increasing dividends year after year.

Strong Stock

While we're sure you've heard the adage "buy low, sell high," you may end up paying top dollar initially for the stocks you choose for your portfolio. Value investing, which looks for beaten-down stocks, won't work for you with direct stock investing. With value investing you want to find cheap stocks. Usually cheap stocks are not currently earning a profit, or profits are down and are not paying dividends, so they don't make a good candidate for direct stock investing.

You want to find those stocks in the strongest position with a bright future for even further growth. Remember, you'll only be able to take advantage of dividend reinvestment if there are significant dividends to reinvest.

Direct Aids

Don't worry too much about a higher price. You may need to save your money for a few months to buy that first share of stock, but it will be worth the wait. Choose your stocks by their long-term potential, not their short-term price.

Industry Domination

Another key factor to consider when picking a long-term stock is its position within the industry. You want to look for stocks that have such a strong position they dominate the industry. For example, Coca-Cola and PepsiCo both dominate the beverage industry. While others fight for position, you're best off choosing a top player when it comes to selecting a good long-term investment.

You might get a better price for a second-tier company, but you can't be sure the company you choose will ever make it to a dominant position. Since you are trying to pick stocks for the long haul to build your portfolio, pick the proven winners—not the wannabes.

You also want to consider the products a company offers. If you believe the dominant player is not watching its competition and you think the number two or three player has much better product offerings that will push it to the dominant role, then by all means consider adding that stock to your portfolio.

This is where your knowledge about the industries in which you choose to invest becomes so critical. You should know the industry and understand how the products in that industry are changing and advancing.

Choose the companies for your portfolio that you know will be there in 10 to 20 years because they are developing products for the future. You can find out about a company's areas of research and development by reading its annual reports, reading articles on its website, and reading articles in industry magazines about research and development.

Yes, picking stocks requires a lot of up-front research, but if you put in the time to do the initial research, you'll be rewarded with a long-term portfolio that will continue to grow.

Managing Your Portfolio

You don't want to put all your eggs in one basket. It's always good to diversify and hold shares in more than one industry. Ultimately, you may want to pick two or three companies in each of the industries you choose to add to your portfolio.

Portfolio managers generally believe that a well-diversified portfolio includes 10 to 20 stocks in several different industries. But don't feel pressured to buy that many stocks up front. Build your portfolio slowly and add stocks as you can afford to do so.

Some industries go up at times that others go down, so by holding a well-diversified group of stocks, you have a much better chance of riding out any economic storm.

How Many Stocks to Buy

All you need to buy directly is one stock per company you choose, then you can apply directly through the company for participation in its DRIP program. We talk more about how to buy that first share of stock in Chapter 4.

If you choose a company that offers a DSP, then you'll be able to make your first purchase directly through the company. We talk more about how to get started with DSPs in the next chapter.

The Least You Need to Know

- Don't waste your time researching all companies. Just research those that offer DSPs or DRIPs.

- Look for defensive industries—those industries that do well in both good and bad times.

- Search for companies with qualities that have shown over the years they will be around for the long haul.

- Diversify your portfolio with 10 to 20 stocks in several different industries to be sure your portfolio can withstand the ups and downs of stock investing.

3

Getting Started with DSPs

In This Chapter

- DSP basics
- Key features
- Buying and selling shares
- Reinvesting dividends

Today, you don't even have to buy a share of stock before you start building a portfolio with direct stock investing, as long as the company has a direct stock purchase (DSP) plan. Some companies call them direct purchase and sale plans. Whatever the name, they work essentially the same way, letting you bypass a broker (not pay commissions) and buy stock directly from the company.

In this chapter, we'll talk about how you can buy stock directly and the basics of setting up an account. Then we'll review the key provisions of DSP accounts.

Basics of DSPs

Investors used to have to buy a share of stock before being able to buy stock directly from a company. Luckily all that changed in the 1990s when the Securities and Exchange Commission (SEC) allowed companies to sell their stock more easily to the public. Prior to that ruling, most direct purchase plans were offered by public utility companies.

Today more than 600 companies offer DSP plans, but you won't find all the detail about a DSP on company websites. To find that detail you'll usually need to go to the administrator's website.

What you can find on a company's website is the name of the *transfer agent* who handles the DSP plan for the company. You'll find that information on the investor relations site, or you can call the company for the name of the transfer agent. The transfer agents are also the account administrators, and we talk about their role in more detail in Chapter 5. Once you know the name of the transfer agent, you can go to that agent's website for more information.

def•i•ni•tion

A **transfer agent** is hired by a corporation to maintain shareholder records, including purchases, sales, and account balances.

Why Companies Offer DSPs

Companies find they can raise capital at a lower cost using DSPs. By encouraging long-term shareholders from the retail sector, companies can not only sell shares cheaper, they can also balance the influence of *institutional investors*.

def•i•ni•tion

> **Institutional investors** are large investors. They can include investment companies, mutual funds, insurance companies, pension funds, investment banks, or endowment funds. They often hold the majority of shares in many companies.

Another reason companies offer DSPs is to gain the support of Main Street America. Companies have found that shareholders with small amounts to invest who don't have enough money to start a brokerage account remain loyal to the brand when they own a bit of the company. So not only do companies get long-term stockholders, they also get long-term customers for their products.

Investors like you get to share in the company's savings because they usually offer you the opportunity to buy shares with low-cost fees, often cheaper than a broker. You can also purchase fractional shares. If you purchase shares from a broker, the minimum number of shares you can buy is one.

For example, if you want to buy a stock that is $50, you would have to give the broker at least $50 to get stock. Using a DSP plan where you buy stocks at the rate of $25 per week, you could get a 50¢ share each time you make an investment.

Watch Out for Fees

When you start looking at DSP plans, you should definitely check out the fees first. Since you're looking to avoid brokerage commissions, you don't want to sign up with a company that makes you pay significant fees every time you invest, especially because you'll likely be investing with small amounts, say $25 to $50, each time. If a company makes you pay $5 each time you send in a check, that would mean 20 percent of all your purchases will be going toward fees. You'd be better off buying that stock through a discount broker and depositing a set amount each week in a money market account until you had enough to buy shares of stock at a lower cost.

Suppose a stock cost $20 per share and you found a broker that will buy shares for you at $9 per transaction. You could buy five shares of stock at a cost of $100 for a transaction fee of $9, or $109 in total. But had you bought the stock through a DSP plan, sending in $25 per week, at the end of four weeks you would have sent in $100 but lost $20 to fees ($5 per week for four weeks), so you'd only have $80 worth of stock, or four shares rather than five.

If a company's fees are high, you might be better off using an account with a discount broker or working with ShareBuilder (www.sharebuilder.com), which lets you buy shares for as low as $4 per transaction. Its stock purchase programs are geared to the small investor.

Key Features You Should Find

You should decide on which companies to buy before you even start comparing feature details. But once you do pick your stocks, you should be certain that a company offers the DSP features you want before you get involved with their plan. If the features that you want are not offered, you'll be better off using a discount broker than buying stock directly from the company's transfer agent.

Here are some key features most direct stock investors want:

- **Convenient purchase options:** With this feature you can make both original and additional cash purchases directly through the company's transfer agent. Additional purchases are called optional cash investments.

- **Automatic dividend reinvestment:** With this feature you can set up your account to have dividends automatically reinvested into additional shares of stock.

- **Certificate or book-entry ownership:** You can own your shares by requesting certificates of stock or by allowing the company to keep track of your shares using book-entry ownership. Most people choose book-entry ownership so they don't have to worry about the safety of the certificates. You will receive statements and confirmations that reflect your transaction history.

- **Deposit of certificated shares:** If you already own shares in the company, you want the right to deposit those share certificates into your direct ownership plan. That way you will be able to reinvest the dividends of the shares you already own as well as the new shares you will be buying.

- **Direct sale:** If a company allows direct sales, the shares can be sold directly without the company having to issue a certificate that you then deposit with a broker in order to sell the shares.

Enrolling in a Plan

Enrollment is usually rather painless. You can call the transfer agent and ask for an enrollment package. You'll get a set of enrollment plans that you must complete and return with your check.

If you want to set up the account with more than one owner, such as a husband and wife or parent and children, all who will be owners of the account must sign the forms.

Most plans have a one-time enrollment fee, so you'll need to send a check for that amount plus the amount of your first purchase. The initial purchase may be higher than subsequent purchases. For example, Colgate-Palmolive requires new shareholders to make an initial investment of $500 in its DSP plan, while existing shareholders can make purchases for as little as $50.

Companies will also usually set a maximum dollar amount you can invest using the stock purchase plan each year. For example, Colgate-Palmolive allows investors to buy up to $10,000 per investment and up to $120,000 in investments per year.

Purchasing Additional Shares

Most companies allow you to buy additional shares through a process called optional share investments. You can usually make these investments by sending a check or doing an electronic funds transfer (EFT). In most cases you will find that the fees for an investment by check are higher than the fees for EFTs, so your best bet is to set up an EFT between your checking account and the transfer agent.

You will likely be given a form as part of the enrollment package that enables you to set up an EFT. You've probably seen these forms when you arrange for a direct deposit of your check at work. Essentially you fill out your identifying information, sign the form, and attach a voided check.

Optional cash investments can be more than double the cost if you work with checks. For example, Colgate-Palmolive charges $1 per investment by EFT plus 10¢ per share purchased. But you'll end up paying $2.50 per investment plus 10¢ per share for investments made by check. That extra $1.50 may not sound like much, but after 12 months you'll pay an extra $18 and after 10 years an extra $180—plus the cost of mailing all those checks. In addition to losing the cash, you'll also own fewer shares of stocks and have gotten less in dividends.

The best way to set up your account is with automatic monthly investments. This type of investing is called dollar-cost averaging. We talk more about why this works so well in Chapter 8.

Many companies charge less per transaction for people who use dollar-cost averaging; others charge the same as the rate for EFT transactions. You'll need to check with a company's transfer agent regarding the company's policy on automatic monthly investments. You can also get the forms needed for automatic monthly investments from the transfer agent.

Reinvesting Dividends

Since reinvesting dividends is not automatic, when you fill out your enrollment form be sure to check the option to automatically reinvest your dividends. It's one of the best ways to build your portfolio without having to come up with cash.

Many companies allow you to reinvest dividends at no cost. Try to build your portfolio primarily with those companies, but as long as the fees are low it can't hurt to include others as well. For example, Colgate-Palmolive charges a service fee of 5 percent of the investment amount with a maximum of $1.25 per dividend payment plus 10¢ per share purchased. At the time of this writing, Colgate-Palmolive's quarterly dividend was 44¢ per share. If you owned 10 shares, that would be $4.40. Multiply that by 5 percent and your fee would be 22¢ plus 10¢ per share bought. Colgate-Palmolive was selling at $71.30 per share at the time of this writing, so you would only be able to buy 0.05804 of a share, but that adds up over time. As your holdings increase, so will your dividend reinvestments.

As your portfolio grows and you get nearer to retirement, you may not want to reinvest all your dividends. You may decide it's time to take out at least part of those dividends for cash needs. Many companies allow you to choose from two types of dividend reinvestment plans:

- **Full dividend investment:** If you pick this option, all your cash dividends on all the shares you own will be used to purchase additional shares.

- **Partial dividend investment:** If you pick this option, you designate the number of shares into which you want cash dividends reinvested.

If you decide not to reinvest your dividends or to reinvest only part of your dividends, you can usually have the dividends wired or electronically transferred to your bank.

Purchasing Shares

When you choose to invest through a DSP plan, the actual purchases are not decided by you. You make your cash investment through the transfer agent, then the transfer agent groups everyone's cash investments and makes periodic purchases of stock. You will not know the price you pay for that stock until after the transfer agent makes the purchase and sends you a transaction verification.

Your per-share purchase price will include the per-share transaction fee and an average weighted price for all shares purchased on that date, plus any transaction fees the agent had to pay. Transfer agents may buy shares daily or once a week, depending on their trading policies.

Your DSP account will be credited for all full and fractional shares (to four decimal places) purchased on your behalf. Purchases with respect to optional cash investments are usually made once per week. Cash dividend purchases are made on the dividend payable date or the day after.

When a company has a lot of cash to invest from DSP account holders, it may decide not to trade all that cash in one day because it can negatively affect the trading price. Instead the company may make the trades over several days, so don't be surprised if it sometimes takes a bit longer to get verification of your transaction.

Selling Your Shares

While you shouldn't use direct stock investing if you're planning to buy and sell shares frequently, you may occasionally need cash and want to sell shares. Many companies offer you three ways to do this:

- **Sale orders via phone:** You can call your company's transfer agent and place a sale order. Most companies will ask for your Social Security number or other identifier to be sure it is you. Many have automated phone systems that will take you through a series of steps to start the sales process. Be sure you have your most recent statement on hand to be able to give your account number and other identifying information.

- **Sale orders via Internet:** Many transfer agents have interactive websites that allow you to log in to your account and set up an order to sell your shares. If you don't regularly use the website to check your account, you may need to set up your online account before you'll be able to sell shares via the Internet.

- **Sale orders via mail:** Many transfer agents include a tear-off portion of the account statement for the purchase or sale of additional shares. You can fill out this form indicating the number of shares you want to sell and send it via snail mail to the transfer agent. This will definitely be the slowest way to get your money.

Even after you place an order to sell shares, you may have to wait a week or two before you see your money. Most transfer agents *aggregate* their sales over a number of days. They then work with an affiliated broker to actually sell the shares, usually once a week.

def•i•ni•tion

> **Aggregate** means to pull together sales from a number of different DSP account holders.

After the sale, you have to wait three days for the trade settlement date and then the transfer agent can process the check. You will have to wait two to three days after the settlement date for a check to be drawn. So from the time you place your sell order it could take about two weeks to actually get the cash.

You won't know the actual sale price until after the sale is complete. And all companies have a fee for selling shares. For example, the fee for Colgate-Palmolive is $15 per transaction plus 10¢ per share.

Yes, it would be cheaper to sell shares through a discount broker, so don't use DSPs if you plan to buy and sell shares regularly. Direct stock investing makes sense only for buy and hold investors.

Transferring Sales to a Broker

You may decide you want to close your DSP and pull all your individual stock holdings under one brokerage firm. You will need to request a transfer package from your transfer agent.

Whenever you plan to transfer shares, you will need to complete a Medallion Signature Guarantee, which guarantees your identity to the transfer agent to be sure no one else takes possession of your shares. The bank in which you have your checking and savings accounts can usually complete the Medallion Signature Guarantee for you.

Closing Your DSP

If you decide you don't want to be part of a DSP anymore and you just want to get copies of your stock certificates, you can probably do that by using the tear-off portion of your most recent account statement, but do check with your transfer agent. Since the agent will be sending the certificates in your name, the Medallion Signature Guarantee will probably not be required.

Purchase Pitfalls

Be very careful if you request stock certificates. They are almost like getting cash and very difficult to replace if lost or stolen. Always put stock certificates in a safe place, such as a safe deposit box at the bank.

Now that we've taken a closer look at DSP accounts, let's move on to how you get started buying your first share of stock for a DRIP.

The Least You Need to Know

- You can buy shares directly from companies, but be sure the fees are low enough or it could end up costing you more to invest than buying stock through discount brokers.

- DSPs allow you to buy fractional shares, which discount brokers do not allow. This permits you to buy shares with small investments each month.

- Reinvesting dividends helps grow your stock holdings more quickly.

- You can typically buy and sell shares by phone, Internet, or mail through transfer agents that manage DSPs for companies.

Chapter **4**

Buying Your First DRIP Share

In This Chapter

- Buying from the company
- Buying from a third-party seller
- Buying from a friend
- Buying from a broker

Getting your first share of stock can be your biggest challenge. You can buy that share directly from the company, if it permits you to do so. You can buy it from a company that specializes in selling just one share. You can get it from a friend, either by gift or purchase. Or, you can do it the most expensive way—buy one share from a stockbroker.

In this chapter, we'll look at the pros and cons of each type of purchase. But whatever way you decide to buy that first share, be certain you get a copy of the participation plan or prospectus from the company so you know all the rules and all the costs of its DRIP before buying that first share.

Buying a Share from the Company

For many years, only a handful of companies allowed shareholders to purchase shares directly. But in 1995, the Securities and Exchange Commission (SEC) eased its regulations, allowing corporations to implement direct purchase programs much more easily.

Since that time, the number of companies that sell first shares directly to investors has grown from a handful to more than 570. Once you own a share of stock, over 1,600 companies then allow you to open a DRIP.

After you buy your first share, companies will allow you to continue to buy shares with additional fees. In fact, some companies will charge different fees depending upon how you choose to do additional investments.

Purchase Pitfalls

Some companies (usually banks or utilities) limit initial purchases to customers or residents. You will always find there are nominal fees or commissions involved. You may also find there is a minimum purchase requirement that ranges from about $200 to $1,000, but many companies will let you start with $0 and buy your first share at the current market price.

For example, American Express, which does require an initial investment of $1,000, allows you to make additional investments for as little as $50. If you make that investment by check or money order, it costs you $5. If you make it by electronic transfer, it costs you $3.50. The cheapest way to buy additional shares is by automatic withdrawal from your account for a cost of $2 per purchase.

Just to give you one other example, Archer-Daniels-Midland Company (ADM) has no minimum investment required, but you must already own at least one share of stock to sign up for their DRIP. You can buy additional shares with additional purchases for as low as $10. There's no charge for dividend reinvestments, but new purchases do have fees depending upon how you complete the purchase. The fees for purchasing ADM shares match those for American Express—$5 for purchase by check, $3.50 by electronic transfer, and $2 by automatic deposit. There is also a 12¢ trading fee per share acquired, so buying only $10 at a time would end up costing you considerable fees and negate any true savings. Read Chapter 11 for information about fees and how they can hurt your investment.

Both plans are administered by the Bank of New York Mellon, which can help you get the first share for companies whose programs they administer. We talk more about that later in the chapter.

Getting a Share from a Third Party

Unless you already own a share or can get one cheaply from a friend, the best way to get your first share is by going through a third party that specializes in direct stock investing. The four most popular places to buy your first share include the National Association of Investors Corporation, First Share, ShareBuilder, and the Bank of New York Mellon.

BetterInvesting

BetterInvesting, formerly known as the National Association of Investors Corporation or NAIC (www.betterinvesting.org), is a not-for-profit organization of investment clubs and individual investors. They offer investment education for both novice and experienced investors.

You can join BetterInvesting for $25 per year, which includes a subscription to *BetterInvesting Magazine*. In addition, you'll get discounts on books, magazines, and investors' analytical and portfolio management software.

But the big advantage for the direct stock investor is the MyStockFund Stock Purchase Plan offered to BetterInvesting members. Through this plan, you can make one free stock purchase each month for the first year of your BetterInvesting membership. Since you won't be paying a commission, this is a low-cost way to begin building up a portfolio of stocks.

First Share

First Share (www.firstshare.com) is a membership organization that facilitates the purchase and sale of an initial share of common stock for companies that offer DRIPs. It matches a First Share member who wishes to buy a stock in a particular company with a member who's willing to sell a single share of stock to another First Share member. All of the companies available through First Share offer a direct purchase program, which allows investors who own a single share of the company's stock to participate in such direct purchase programs.

First Share maintains a database of members who own shares in the companies qualified for the First Share program and who have offered to sell single shares to other members. When a member submits a request to First Share to purchase one share of a company, First Share refers the request to members who may be willing to sell a share of the company requested. When a match is found, First Share mails confirmation of the request to the purchasing member with the name and address information of the selling member and the name and telephone number of the company's DRIP administrator.

The seller contacts the purchaser by forwarding a written offer to sell a single share at a specified price plus a small handling fee for the seller's expenses. Upon receipt of the accepted offer and registration information from the purchaser, plus the agreed price of the share and the handling fee, the seller forwards the registration information to the company's stock transfer agent.

The company's stock transfer agent registers one share in the purchaser's name and forwards a stock certificate to the purchaser, or opens a DRIP account in the purchaser's name. After the share is registered, the purchaser may enroll in the company's direct stock purchase plan or dividend reinvestment plan. Once a member owns a share of stock, all future transactions are made directly through the company's plan.

After a member has purchased a company through First Share, he or she is obligated to sell a share to another member at some time in the future.

ShareBuilder

ShareBuilder (www.sharebuilder.com) is an online brokerage designed to make investing easy, affordable, and accessible for both beginning and experienced investors. ShareBuilder offers a full range of services, including automatic investing that allows you to buy stocks in whole dollar amounts.

ShareBuilder also offers an automatic investment plan that allows you to buy stocks through automatic, scheduled purchases. Invest any dollar amount weekly, biweekly, or monthly. Select stocks that interest you from the over 7,000 offered, but remember only about 880 have DRIPs.

You can invest as much or as little as you choose; there is no account minimum. With a Basic account, each investment costs $4, but there are no monthly subscription costs. With the Standard ($12 per month) and Advantage ($20 per month) accounts, automatic investments are included as a part of the monthly subscription. With Standard, your first 6 are included, and with Advantage, your first 20 are included at no extra charge.

Bank of New York Mellon

The Bank of New York Mellon's Investor Services Direct (https://vault.bnymellon.com/isd/ Default.asp?PLID=BNYM) makes it easy for investors to buy the first share of stock plus additional shares of stock for the companies whose direct stock programs it administers. When you get to the website, click on "Investment Plan Enrollment" to search the available plans and download plan enrollment details for all the companies the bank handles. If you ask for an alphabetical list, you'll find about 550 companies from which to choose.

Even if you don't plan to purchase through the Bank of New York Mellon, you'll find it much easier to get the plan documents using its online research tool.

The costs and required initial investment differs for each program depending on the plan documents. We have summarized plans for some of the top companies (not only those administered by Mellon) in Appendix B.

Getting a Share from a Friend

Your cheapest way to buy a share will likely be to get a single share from a friend, but it does require a significant amount of paperwork. If you have a friend who owns stock in a DRIP, you can arrange to purchase a single share. Your friend can charge a nominal commission, and you'll need to pay the market price of the share plus any additional transfer charges (if there are any).

Some companies make it easy by allowing the transfer of a single share into a new DRIP account with just a signed enrollment form. In other cases, a cumbersome share-transfer process will have to be followed.

- A DRIP owner would notify the company's transfer agent to transfer a single share of stock to the buyer.

- The share owner would need to complete a "stock power," or sign the back of the share certificate.

- Be sure to sign the "stock power" or "stock certificate" in front of a bank officer who can guarantee the owner's signature. The guarantee must be a participant in the Medallion Signature Guarantee program of the Securities Transfer Association. Your friend who is selling the share can usually find someone to guarantee the signature at his or her bank. You can also find someone who can guarantee a signature at most brokerage houses. In either case, a bank or brokerage house may only guarantee signatures for people who have active accounts.

- The signed stock power or certificate is then sent to the transfer agent, with a letter of intent describing the transfer that is to occur.

- Expect the process to take four to eight weeks before the buyer receives the certificate or statement from the DRIP administrator.

Direct Aids

You may be wondering where you can get a stock power form. Luckily that is not usually a difficult task. Most transfer agents and DRIP administrators can provide a stock power form that you can use. Often, these forms are published on their websites.

Buying a Share from a Stockbroker

You're probably most familiar with the idea of purchasing stock through a brokerage house, but that's not usually your best bet when you just need to buy one share. Full-service brokers often don't want the hassle of selling and issuing a certificate for a single share of stock.

If you feel most comfortable buying stock from a broker, then your best bet will be deep-discount online brokers, such as E*TRADE or TD Ameritrade.

Commissions at deep-discount online brokers are now under $10 per trade, so it's not as costly to buy just one share. But you may face other fees, such as charges to have stock certificates issued to the owner rather than having the broker hold them in *street name.*

def•i•ni•tion

Street name means the stock is registered in the name of your brokerage firm on the issuer's books. Your brokerage firm holds the security for you in "book-entry" form. Book-entry simply means that you do not receive a certificate. Instead, your broker keeps a record in their books that you own that particular security.

Using a deep-discount broker, you can purchase one or more shares, and then enroll in a corporation's DRIP. But you may find that even discount brokers require a $500 to $1,000 minimum deposit to establish an online account. So if you don't have enough money to buy your first share with a broker, consider joining BetterInvesting or working with ShareBuilder or First Share, as discussed previously.

Holding On to the Stock

You can hold a stock in one of three ways: physical certificate, street name registration, and direct registration. Here's a brief overview of each.

Physical Certificate

You always have the right to ask your broker or the company from which you are buying a share of stock to get actual stock certificates sent to you. You may have to pay a fee for the added expense of issuing a paper certificate. Fees can be $50 to $75 and in some cases as high as $500.

If you do get a stock certificate, be sure to safeguard it until you sell or transfer your securities. It can be difficult to prove that you once owned a certificate that has been lost, stolen, or destroyed. Your broker—or the company or its transfer agent—will generally charge a fee to replace a lost or stolen stock certificate.

The advantages of holding a physical certificate include:

- The company knows how to reach you and will send all company reports and other information to you directly.
- You may find it easier to pledge your securities as collateral for a loan if you hold the certificates yourself in physical certificate form.

But there are disadvantages as well:

- When you want to sell your stock, you will have to send the certificate to your broker or the company's transfer agent to execute the sale. This may make it harder for you to sell quickly.

- If you lose your certificate, you may be charged a fee for a replacement.
- If you move, you will have to contact the company with your change of address so that you do not miss any important mailings.

Street Name Registration

Most people buy stock through a broker and the stock is held as a street name registration. This gives you greater security, and your stockbroker is the primary contact with the company. However, you can't use this form of registration if you want to set up a DRIP account.

Many brokerage firms will automatically put your securities into street name unless you give them specific instructions to the contrary. Under street name registration, your firm will keep records showing you as the real or "beneficial" owner, but you will not be listed directly on the issuer's books. Instead, your brokerage firm (or some other nominee) will appear as the owner on the issuer's books.

While you will not receive a certificate, your firm will send to you, at least four times a year, an account statement that lists all your securities at the broker. Your broker will also credit your account with your dividend and interest payments and will provide you with consolidated tax information. Your broker-dealer will send you issuer mailings, such as annual reports and proxies.

If you're not planning to buy stock directly from the company, there are many advantages to this form of stock registration:

- Since your securities are already with your broker, you can more easily sell the stock.

- Your brokerage firm is responsible for safeguarding your securities certificates so you don't have to worry about those certificates being lost or stolen.

- Your brokerage firm may keep you informed of important developments, such as stock splits and dividend payouts.

But there are disadvantages to street name registration. These include:

- You may experience a slight delay in receiving your dividend and interest payments from your brokerage firm. For example, some firms only pass along these payments to investors on a weekly, biweekly, or monthly basis.

- Since your name is not on the books of the company, the company will not mail important corporate communications directly to you.

Direct Registration

You most likely will use direct registration when you open a DSP or DRIP account with a company. Your stock ownership will be registered directly on the books of the company, regardless of whether you bought your securities through your broker or directly from the company or its transfer agent through a direct investment plan.

Direct registration allows you to have your security registered in your name on the books of the issuer without the need for a physical certificate to serve as evidence of your ownership. While you will not receive a certificate, you will receive a statement of ownership and periodic account statements, dividends, annual reports, proxies, and other mailings directly from the issuer.

The primary advantages of direct registration include:

- Since you are "registered" on the books of the company as the shareholder, you will receive annual and other reports, dividends, proxies, and other communications directly from the company.

- If you want to sell your securities through your broker, you can instruct your broker to electronically move your securities from the books of the company and then to sell your securities. Your broker should be able to do this quickly without the need for you filling out complicated and time-consuming forms.

- You do not have to worry about safekeeping or losing certificates, or having them stolen.

But there are disadvantages as well:

- If you choose to buy or sell registered securities through a company's direct investment plan, you usually will not be able to buy or sell at a specific market price or at a specific time.

- Most companies purchase or sell shares for the plan at established times—for example, on a daily, weekly, or monthly basis—and at an average market price.

Now that we've reviewed the many different ways you can buy your first share of stock, let's take a look at how to open your DSP or DRIP account directly with a company.

The Least You Need to Know

- You may be able to buy your first share directly from a company, but not all corporations offer that option right now.

- Several good third-party sellers can help you get your first share of stock for a reasonable price.

- Each option has pros and cons, so do your research carefully to see which works best for you.

- You can hold your shares in several different ways, but the safest way to hold shares when you're doing DRIP investing is by direct registration.

Chapter 5

Setting Up a DRIP Account

In This Chapter

- Account setup
- Eligibility requirements
- Transaction fees
- Buying, transferring, and selling shares

Now that you've purchased your first share or shares, you need to set up a DRIP account with the company. An administrator outside the company manages most DRIP accounts. We talk more about administrators and their role in the next chapter.

In this chapter, we take a closer look at how to set up your DRIP account and what account features you want to look for as you pick companies for your DRIP portfolio.

Establishing Your Account

Your stock may be set up electronically with the company or you may have stock certificates in hand. If you have chosen to use certificates when purchasing your first shares, be sure you keep those certificates in a safe place. As you build up the required number of shares, your best bet is to put them in a bank safety deposit box, but if you don't have one, you can use a fireproof safe in your home. You also can set up direct registration with the company rather than hold on to your certificates, as discussed in Chapter 4.

Direct Aids _____

Each company sets its own requirements for the number of shares that must be owned. For example, Consolidated Edison requires that you own 50 shares of stock before you can apply for the DRIP program.

You don't have to worry too much about your certificate being stolen. A thief would find it relatively difficult to transfer shares into his or her name, but the costs and hassles involved in replacing lost or stolen certificates can take up a lot of unnecessary time and money.

With your shares in hand, you're ready to establish a DRIP account with the company. How you do that will depend on how you bought your first share or shares. Some enrollment services actually transfer the single share into a new account with the participating DRIP company. In other cases, such as purchasing a single share through First Share, you may receive an actual stock certificate and then must enroll directly with the company.

Even if the company from which you bought your first share handles the paperwork for you, it's best to call or write the company and request a copy of the DRIP prospectus and enrollment form.

Direct Aids

Carefully examine the prospectus so you can clearly understand the rules for all costs associated with reinvesting dividends or making additional cash investments.

The prospectus will outline the schedule for optional cash purchases and reinvestment of dividends, fees, or commissions involved with buying or selling shares, as well as other pertinent information. You may be able to access the DRIP enrollment form and prospectus on a company's website, or by calling the company's investor relations office or transfer agent and requesting that a copy be sent by mail. In some cases you can also download the needed information from the transfer agent (administrator) for the plan.

You'll find the actual DRIP enrollment form very straightforward. You'll need to complete lines asking for the name of the account holder, Social Security or taxpayer identification number, contact information, date, and signature. You may also find you have options for how you can participate in the DRIP, such as:

- Reinvesting dividends fully
- Reinvesting dividends partially and asking for some portion of dividends to be paid in cash

- No dividend reinvestments, just additional cash investments through the optional cash purchases provisions

Reinvesting dividends fully is the most common way to take full advantage of DRIPs. That way your portfolio grows without laying out any additional money. You can always make additional cash investments, too.

If the DRIP offers direct debit purchases (in which money will be automatically transferred from your bank account on a regular basis to invest in additional shares of stock), you will get a separate form to set up this feature. You will need to attach a voided check so the administrator has your account information. The form will also ask you to specify the amount you'd like to invest regularly on this form.

Direct Aids

Take advantage of these automatic debit plans to automatically build your portfolio without any extra work. You'll invest regularly and be able to take full advantage of dollar-cost averaging, which we talk about in more detail in Chapter 8. Direct debit plans are an easy way to invest on a regular basis, and you'll never forget to make your monthly investment in the plan.

You can set up your DRIP account using several different forms of ownership, depending on your preference. The most common forms of ownership include:

- **Individual:** You are the sole owner of the account.

- **Joint tenants:** You name more than one owner of the account and both of you share ownership of the stock. This is a common form of ownership for husband and wife.

- **Minor ownership:** You set up the account for a minor, such as your child or grand-child. You will need to name the minor as well as a custodian for the minor, who in most cases will be yourself. You will need a Social Security number for the child, as well as for yourself.

- **Trusts:** You will need the name of the trustee as well as the recipient of the trust. You should set this up with an attorney prior to filling out the DRIP form.

- **Partnership:** This form of ownership is for a group of unrelated people. Investment clubs that own DRIP accounts usually use this type of ownership.

If you do plan to give or purchase stock for your minor children or grandchildren, you must name a custodian because minors cannot legally own stock directly. When you set up the account, you can name the child as the account owner, but the custodian controls the account until the child is no longer legally a minor.

Stock Facts

All states, except South Carolina and Vermont, have adopted the Uniform Transfers to Minors Act (UTMA) to govern the transfer of ownership of property to children. South Carolina and Vermont have a similar provision called the Uniform Gift to Minors Act (UGMA).

Both Uniform Transfers to Minors Act (UTMA) and Uniform Gift to Minors Act (UGMA) accounts limit the minor's access to the account until he or she reaches the age of majority as set by state law, typically from 18 to 21 years of age. The reason people choose to use these plans is because they offer favorable tax treatment of investment earnings. We'll talk more about tax benefits in Chapter 12.

DRIP Advantages

As you look at DRIPs, consider what types of advantages you'll need. You can find details in the prospectus. Here are some key features you want to look for:

- You should not have to pay brokerage fees to buy additional shares. You may have to pay a processing fee for additional cash purchases, but make sure these fees are lower than what you would pay a discount broker.

- You should be able to reinvest dividends easily and automatically.

- You should be able to buy fractions of shares. That's a big advantage of a DRIP over a brokerage house. With a brokerage house, the least you can buy is one share, so often your money sits in a money market account until you have enough money to buy a share. With a DRIP you can buy a fraction of a share and continue to build your stock ownership with each dividend payout.

Plan Eligibility

Each company decides on an administrator for its DRIP, which is usually a bank. The bank maintains an account for each participant to record transactions under the plan. The bank also buys and sells stocks for participants.

The administrator also holds shares of stock as the custodian for participants. We talk more about account administrators and what they do in Chapter 6.

Each company sets its own rules for DRIP eligibility. As part of its eligibility requirements, a plan will specify:

- The number of shares you must own before becoming eligible to apply for participation in the DRIP.

- If you don't own all the shares in your name, the eligibility requirements will specify how to transfer ownership of the shares to your name. This can also be a factor if a broker holds your certificates and you must transfer ownership.

- Whether you can participate in the DRIP if you are not a U.S. citizen. Some companies will have special rules for non–U.S. citizens; others will just specify that your participation in the program cannot violate the local laws of the country in which you live or have citizenship.

Purchase Pitfalls

As you research potential stock candidates for your portfolio, be sure you check on the number of shares you must own before you can sign up for the plan. If the company requires too many shares, you may want to pick another company in the same industry, as long as you think the long-term potential is strong.

Additional Investments

After you set up your DRIP account, most companies allow you to make additional cash investments in the plan as well as reinvest your dividends. Check the costs and rules for making additional cash investments.

In most cases a company will specify the maximum or minimum allowable amounts of cash investments monthly and yearly. For example, Consolidated Edison allows people enrolled in its DRIP to make additional cash investments of at least $100 per payment but does not allow investments of more than $100,000 in any one year. The company charges $2 to process new cash investments.

> ### Purchase Pitfalls
>
> As you research your potential candidates, be sure to find out the charges for new cash investments. Compare them to what you would pay for new shares using an online broker. Sometimes you may decide to make less frequent purchases if charges for new cash investments eat up too much of your investment.

New cash investments may not be used to buy stock the same day you send in your money. For example, Consolidated Edison tells its DRIP participants that "cash payments will be invested weekly by the Bank; no interest will be paid to participants on cash payments held pending investment. There is no obligation to make cash payments."

The Bank of New York Mellon is the administrator for Consolidated Edison, and it indicates that it buys stock about once a week, pooling all new investments from DRIP participants. Participants can make new investments by sending a check.

Electronic funds transfers (EFTs) are not allowed in the Consolidated Edison plan, but you may find that other plans do accept them.

What's the Source of the Shares?

You may be wondering where the shares of stock you purchase originate. In some cases the stock will be from shares that were authorized by the board of directors but not yet issued. In other cases the administrator for the company's DRIP will buy shares on the open market through an affiliated broker.

If shares are bought on the open market, the purchases of all new DRIP investors are pooled and may be made over a number of days to minimize any impact on the stock's selling price.

You won't know the price you actually paid for the stock until after you get the transaction information from the DRIP administrator. This is very different from buying stock through an online broker, where you actually know the price within seconds of placing the order. But you are buying stock for the long haul, so minor fluctuations in price should not have a major impact on your portfolio. Since you are buying from long-established blue-chip companies, you probably won't see a dramatic price change in stock price over a one- or two-day period that would greatly affect what you pay for the new shares.

For example, Consolidated Edison tells its participants that the price they will pay for their shares will depend on the source of the shares. If the shares are purchased directly from Consolidated Edison, then the share price will be an average of the high and low at which the stock sold that day. If the shares are purchased on the open market, the price paid will be an average of the price paid in that week's transactions.

Cash Dividend Reinvestments

If you authorize your dividends to be reinvested— which you should do unless you really need the cash—new shares will be bought in a process similar to new cash investments. Most people who set up a DRIP account do so because dividends can be reinvested at little or no cost.

Stock Facts

After a dividend is paid, don't expect to see new shares in your account immediately. Since companies often have to buy the new shares on the open market using cash from the dividend payout, it can take a week or more for the shares to be deposited in your account.

When companies are buying shares using a large dividend payout, they can negatively influence the stock price if they try to buy too many shares on the same day. For example, Consolidated Edison tells investors in its DRIP that "cash dividends will be invested not more than five business days after the dividend is paid; no interest will be paid to participants on dividends held pending investment."

The number of shares added to your account will depend on the cash dividend and the share price on the day the administrator buys the new shares. Your account will be credited in whole and fractional shares to reflect your cash dividend reinvestment.

Taxes will also be withheld on any dividends reinvested unless you fill out a form with the administrator indicating you are not subject to federal income tax. We'll talk more about tax implications and DRIPs in Chapter 12.

Transferring Shares Held

You can transfer shares you hold to another participant in the plan or to a participant who will be new to the plan, provided they meet the plan's eligibility requirements. You contact your plan administrator for the necessary forms. When you do make a transfer, you'll receive a transaction confirmation, as will the person to whom you are transferring.

Costs for transferring shares vary by company. Most companies require you to complete a Medallion Signature Guarantee in order to complete the transfer. You will get a Medallion Signature Guarantee as part of a transfer packet from your DRIP administrator. Your bank will be able to help you with completing the signature guarantee.

Selling Shares

The process for selling shares is similar to that for transferring shares. You will need to notify your DRIP administrator that you want to sell shares and ask for whatever forms are necessary to complete the sale of shares.

If the administrator holds your shares using direct registration, the process will be easy. If you hold the certificates, you will need to provide those certificates to the administrator in order for him or her to complete the sale.

Fees are usually higher for selling shares than they are for transferring shares. For example, Consolidated Edison charges a transaction fee of $10 plus 10¢ per share. That may be slightly higher than the cost of a transaction using a discount broker, which could be as low as $8 per transaction, but not so high that you would want to avoid using Consolidated's DRIP program.

Remember that DRIPs are for long-term investing. If you don't plan to hold the stock for years, you shouldn't be considering DRIPs.

Now that you know how to set up a DRIP account, let's take a closer look at the role of DRIP and DSP administrators.

The Least You Need to Know

- Carefully research the fees of each DRIP you are considering to be sure they will not hurt your long-term investing plans.

- You should verify your eligibility for a DRIP before buying shares of stock.

- You have many options for how you want to structure your DRIP. Know those options and which one will work best for you.

- You can reinvest fully or partially any dividends you earn, but you must make your DRIP administrator aware of your plans when you sign up for a DRIP.

Chapter 6

Account Administrators

In This Chapter

- Transfer agent's role
- Account management
- Additional functions

When you set up a DRIP or DSP account, you most likely won't be working directly with the company you've chosen. Instead most companies work with transfer agents who handle their account administration needs. Your account administrator will help you to buy and sell shares, reinvest dividends, vote your shares, track your account, and complete other activities related to stock ownership. In this chapter, we'll review the primary services transfer agents offer corporations and how you can use these services.

Why Companies Choose Transfer Agents

Most public or private companies with shareholders decide to work with a professional transfer agent to act as custodian for their shareholder accounts and to handle any changes in shareholder ownership. Managing shareholder accounts requires purchasing the necessary software to handle the processing and recordkeeping, as well as hiring staff with account administration expertise in corporate securities and compliance.

Meeting Securities and Exchange Commission (SEC) compliance when it comes to account administration can be a job in itself. Most corporations prefer to hire a specialist so they can avoid any compliance problems with the SEC.

In addition to staff issues, account administration of the hundreds of thousands of stockholder accounts is an expensive undertaking. Transfer agents can lower that cost because they maintain the staff, software, and other necessary tools for multiple companies.

So don't be surprised if you're given a contact number for another company when you call the investor relations department. You'll most likely work directly with the transfer agent to set up your stock account, reinvest your dividends, buy and sell shares, and do any other activities related to your stock ownership.

Managing Your DRIP and DSP Accounts

Transfer agents offer a range of DRIP and DSP services. Most give you numerous ways to make additional cash payments and numerous ways to manage your account online. When you contact a transfer agent, be sure to specify the company that interests you because transfer agents represent hundreds and sometimes thousands of companies.

Services they offer you include ...

- The ability to enroll in a DRIP or DSP over the Internet.
- Electronic funds transfer (EFT) services that allow you to transfer funds between your bank accounts and your DRIP or DSP account, as long as the prospectus of the company whose stock you own permits the transfer.
- Internet access to dividend and DRIP and DSP historical information.
- The ability to make periodic optional cash payments.

A number of transfer agents allow you to research DRIPs and DSPs online for the companies in which they handle account administration. At these company websites you can download a prospectus and forms for setting up an account. You can also find a summary of charges for their various services. The four companies that make it easy to research DRIPs and DSPs are American Stock Transfer, Bank of New York Mellon, Computershare, Registrar and Transfer Company, and Wells Fargo.

American Stock Transfer

American Stock Transfer (AST; www.investpower.com) was founded in 1970 and has grown to be the largest independent stock transfer agents in the nation. They serve more than 2,500 companies and some major DRIPs including Microsoft, Dell, Yum Brands, Paychex, and ADP. You can find a complete list of the DRIPs and DSPs administered by AST at www.amstock.com/investpower/new_plandet2.asp.

For shareholder information, call 1-800-937-5449. For dividend reinvestment information, call 1-800-278-4353.

You can contact them by snail mail at:

American Stock Transfer
59 Maiden Lane
Plaza Level
New York, NY 10038

Bank of New York Mellon

The Bank of New York (BNY)/Mellon (www.melloninvestor.com/isd) is the administrator for 547 companies that offer DRIP or DSP options. You can view plan summary, plan material, and compare plans. If the company allows, you can even start your investment online. That option does vary by company, however, and not every company allows online transactions.

You can enroll online 24 hours a day, seven days a week, at www.melloninvestor.com/isd. You should be certain to download and review the prospectus before opening any account. Then complete the application carefully, because if you make a mistake in filling out the application form or fail to include critical information, your application could be delayed.

If you're not comfortable with opening an account online, you can also request an enrollment kit by calling the BNY/Mellon's toll-free number: 1-800-522-6645. You can also request a prospectus and application via e-mail: shrrelations@mellon.com.

If you prefer snail mail, you can write to BNY/Mellon. If you already have an account, you should include your investor identification number in your correspondence. In many cases this will be your Social Security number. But if you are not sure of your investor identification number, call the investor relations department of the company whose shares you own. If you're not yet an investor and are looking to make your first purchase as part of a DSP plan, you can just write a general letter asking for a prospectus and the forms needed to open an account.

Regular mail:

BNY/Mellon Shareowner Services
PO Box 358010
Pittsburgh, PA 15252

Registered or overnight mail:

BNY/Mellon Shareowner Services
480 Washington Boulevard, 27th floor
Jersey City, NJ 07310

Computershare

Computershare (https://www-us.computershare.com) provides transfer services for over 10,000 companies worldwide, and hundreds of them do offer DRIPs and DSPs. In order to find a telephone number for information about a specific company, you'll need to research the information online at https://www-us.computershare.com/Investor/Plans/buyshares.asp. You can also reach Computershare by snail mail at:

Computershare Investor Services
PO Box 43078
Providence, RI 02940

Registrar and Transfer Company

The Registrar and Transfer Company is the transfer agent for over 150 companies that offer DRIPs. You can research companies at www.rtco.com/inv/drp.asp and download plan prospectuses and enrollment forms.

If you don't want to request information online, you can review the list of companies and call for information about the companies that interest you at 1-800-368-5948, or you can send snail mail to the investor relations department at:

Registrar and Transfer Company
ATTN: Investor Relations Department
10 Commerce Drive
Cranford, NJ 07016

Wells Fargo

Wells Fargo administers over 100 dividend reinvestment and direct purchase plans that you can research online at www.wellsfargo.com/com/ shareowner_services/services_for_shareholders/ investment_plans. In addition to DRIP and DSP plans, Wells Fargo administers over 80 employee stock purchase plans.

Always be sure that you download and read each plan's prospectus or brochure before investing because each plan is unique. DSPs are available to all investors, but you must own shares as a registered owner prior to enrolling in a DRIP through Wells Fargo or any account administrator.

If you don't want to download information, you may obtain plan material and enrollment forms by contacting shareowner services at 1-800-401-1957.

You can also contact Wells Fargo using snail mail at:

Shareowner Services
PO Box 64874
St. Paul, MN 55164-0874

These are not the only transfer agents, but they are the only ones that offer you the opportunity to research available plans online before you are a stockholder with one of the companies they serve.

If the corporation that you're interested in opening an account with does not work with one of these three transfer agents, you'll be given the contact information so you can get a copy of the prospectus and application forms.

Other key transfer agents include:

- Continental Stock Transfer (www.continentalstock.com). For more information, you can call Continental Stock Transfer at 212-509-4000.

- Corporate Stock Transfer (www.corporatestock.com). Depending on your question, you can find numerous direct-dial numbers at www.corporatestock.com/contact.

Other Transfer Agent Functions

In addition to serving as DRIP and DSP account administrators for corporations, transfer agents provide other services for corporations that you will want to take advantage of as a stockholder. Let's review some of those other services.

Proxy and Meeting Services

When you own shares in a company, you get the right to vote on issues related to the operations of that company using what is called a proxy. You use a proxy to vote if you don't plan to attend the company meeting. You also have the right to attend the corporation's annual meeting.

Often the transfer agent handles all the needed functions related to proxies and annual meetings, including setting the *proxy record date*, printing materials, tallying proxies, broker searches, and attendance at the meeting as the inspector of election.

def•i•ni•tion

> The **proxy record date** is set by the company; you must own shares of stock on that date in order to vote on a company issue of concern to stockholders.

The process for voting of proxies begins with notification. After the corporation notifies its transfer agent of the record date, the transfer agent arranges for telephone and Internet voting of proxies.

The transfer agent will then produce a shareholder list based on the date of record supplied for the company. The company will need to specify who gets to vote and attend the annual meetings based on a specific date. Since shares are bought and sold daily, people who are shareholders as of a certain date specified by the company will be the only ones who get to vote at that year's annual meeting.

You don't have to actually attend the annual meeting to vote. You will also be able to vote by telephone or Internet, if the transfer agent provides those services. Some transfer agents don't offer telephone and Internet voting. If that is the case for a stock you own, then you'll need to send back the paper ballot you'll get in the mail.

When shareholders send back their proxies, the transfer agent examines the proxies for accuracy and shareholder comments and then calculates the votes. Votes obtained via the Internet or by telephone are automatically entered into the system.

Prior to the annual meeting, the transfer agent submits a report to the company's board of directors that summarizes all voting results. A final vote total is provided to company officials at the meeting. If the company so desires, the transfer agent also provides an experienced Inspector of Elections at its annual meeting to manage voting and provide final results.

The transfer agent is also responsible for keeping a record of the results of the proxy vote along with other documentation in the company's file.

Internet Services

Transfer agents manage the corporation's Internet services for stockholders. Most allow you to access your account and give you the ability to review (and possibly change) the following: full shareholder profile, complete share holdings, dividend payment and check payment history, dividend reinvestment history, ability to change your address and update your account, ability to send e-mails related to your account, tax and withholding information, and W-2 forms.

In addition to your ability to check your accounts, corporations can access your information for various analytical and statistical reports, including shareholder summaries and DRIP or DSP analysis of existing accounts.

Escheatment Services

Sometimes stock holdings are abandoned. Most times this happens after the death of a stockholder. Transfer agents must deal with these situations as well. These services are called escheatment services.

The escheatment process starts after an account is noted as "lost." This typically occurs after mail is returned and it cannot be successfully redelivered.

When that happens, the account is flagged and any property due to the holder is held. Sometimes a flag is easily removed if the account holder sends information about an address change.

Once an account has been flagged as "lost," under SEC regulations the transfer agent has the responsibility to search for a more current address. If the transfer agent can't find a current address for the stockholder, it will be considered "abandoned," and state escheatment regulations will be followed. Each state sets up its own requirements for how to handle abandoned properties.

All states require companies to report escheatment on a yearly basis. As part of this report, the transfer agent lists all of the accounts subject to escheatment, along with all unclaimed property belonging to someone whose last address was known to be in that particular state.

Property abandoned by any foreign account and accounts with incomplete addresses (no state of residence listed) is escheated to the state of incorporation of the issuing company. Transfer agents send a final escheatment report to corporations for their records as well.

If a family member died and the property has been escheated, it may be claimed by the estate of the shareholder. Contact the transfer agent in writing to begin the process of claiming the account. The transfer agent will then let you know which state holds the escheated property and how to make a claim for that property.

Transfer agents do a lot more than serve as DRIP and DSP account administrators, and as a stockholder you'll likely need some of these services as well.

Now let's take a closer look at the type of reports you can expect from the account administrator.

The Least You Need to Know

- Account administration is a complex task that requires careful compliance with SEC rules, so most companies hire a transfer agent to administer their DRIP and DSP accounts.

- Many account administrators make it possible for you to manage your DRIP and DSP accounts online, by telephone, and by mail.

- In addition to managing your accounts, transfer agents manage proxy voting and annual meeting attendance and voting.

- Transfer agents also handle the escheatment process if an account is abandoned.

Reading Your Direct Stock Account Reports

In This Chapter

- Delving into statements
- Optional and automatic investments
- Partial investing options
- Building a spreadsheet

As a DRIP or DSP investor, you will receive statements quarterly (or whenever dividends are usually paid). You'll also get a statement whenever there is activity on your account. In this chapter, we'll review what to look for in statements from your DRIP or DSP. Then we'll discuss the type of recordkeeping you need to do to manage your portfolio.

What's in the Statements?

Your DRIP or DSP statements usually will detail the activity in the account for the year-to-date. You'll find information about any commissions paid to purchase shares or other fees that may have been charged to the account or paid by the company on your behalf.

Typically you'll get a statement when:

- You purchase additional shares
- Your dividends are reinvested
- You sell shares
- You transfer shares
- Quarterly reports on your account
- Year-end reports on your account

Remember, your statements will show whole shares and fractional shares. One big advantage of DRIP and DSP investing is that you don't have to wait until you can afford to buy one share of stock—you can buy a fraction of a share at any time. This can make your report look a bit more confusing and your recordkeeping more difficult, so pay close attention to the fractional shares.

When you get the statement, in addition to information about any transactions, you'll get information about the next date for optional purchases. This will include the date by which your check must be received in order to be included in that round of purchases.

You may even get a postage-paid business envelope. Some companies pick up the cost of sending checks for optional purchases to encourage stock purchases.

Hold on to all statements that you get. You will need them for tax filing at the end of the year. You should also keep all records of stock purchases until after you sell the stock, so you'll have proof of how much you paid for each share of stock. Once you sell the stock, you should wait at least three years before tossing the statements because the IRS may decide to audit your tax return.

This includes information about dividend reinvestments plus optional or automatic cash purchases. As your dividends are reinvested each year, you will be paying taxes on those dividends. But if you can't prove that you bought shares with cash from those dividends, you'll end up paying capital gains on money already taxed as dividends. You need to keep careful records of your actual cost basis for all your DRIP and DSP shares.

We'll talk more about taxes in Chapter 12, but we'll show you how to use a spreadsheet program to track purchases—whether by dividends or additional cash investments—later in the chapter.

Purchase Additional Shares

Another big advantage of opening DRIP and DSP accounts is that you can make additional purchases with little or no commission. These purchases are known as optional cash purchases (OCPs). Companies usually fill OCPs for account holders on a set schedule.

For example, a company may purchase and sell shares for all DRIP or DSP account holders on the business day closest to the 15th of each month. You can find out the schedule for sales and purchases in the DRIP or DSP prospectus. In addition, you can find out the deadline on which cash must arrive in order for the DRIP or DSP administrator to make the purchase for that month.

Direct Aids

Always try to send your OCPs a few days early to be sure you don't miss investment day. If you miss the day stock is purchased, your new investment may be held until the next month.

You'll find there are fees and commissions on all OCPs, but they do vary widely, so always check your statement to find out how much you were charged.

Purchase Pitfalls

Some companies will raise fees on DRIP and DSP transactions, so you must always keep a close watch on your statements. If fees increase constantly, compare those costs to the costs of maintaining a portfolio at an online discount broker. Your DRIP or DSP should always be cheaper to maintain than a brokerage account.

Compare the fees and commissions charged on all the different DRIPs and DSPs you own on a regular basis. You may see that one or two of the companies in which you hold stock continually raise those fees. If they do, you may want to reconsider your choice to hold the shares within the DSP or DRIP.

Dividend Reinvestment

You should always get a statement when dividends are reinvested. For most companies this will be on a quarterly basis. As with the optional cash investments, keep a close watch on the commissions and fees charged.

Sell Shares

You will get a statement after you sell shares once the transaction is complete. Before you even think of selling shares, be sure you check out the current commissions and fees for the sale. In most cases, a DRIP or DSP administrator can handle the sale for you cheaper than a broker.

As a DRIP or DSP investor you are not likely to sell shares regularly, so the cost of these rare transactions should not have a major impact on your profits. But do keep track of the fees on your DRIP and DSP statements because you'll need them when you file your taxes. The fees can be written off, so you can lower any capital gains taxes you must pay. We talk more about that in Chapter 12.

Transfer Shares

You may decide to transfer shares to family members so that they can start their own DRIP or DSP. After you make arrangements for the transfer, watch for a statement that indicates when the transfer was complete and how much it cost you.

Most DRIPs and DSPs do charge administrative fees to transfer shares to someone else, but they are minimal. Keep track of these fees.

Quarterly Reports on Your Account

You should get quarterly reports on your accounts that show all year-to-date transactions. Double check these reports to be sure all the transactions you've made are recorded.

It's rare that something is left off the report, but it's a lot easier to correct a problem if you catch it during the same quarter than if you try to correct it a year or two down the road.

Direct Aids

Always check your statements, and if you find a difference from the account totals you were expecting. Double check every transaction to be sure it has been included in the annual report. You'll find it much easier to correct a problem the faster you report the problem to the company.

Year-End Reports on Your Account

Every DRIP and DSP administrator sends out year-end reports that should reflect all the transactions during the year, as well as a cumulative total of all the shares you own. Check this year-end report against your own records and be sure your holdings match those stated on the annual report.

Tracking Partial DRIP and OCP-Only Options

Some DRIP and DSP companies allow shareholders to designate that only a portion of the regular dividends be reinvested, and the remainder paid in cash. Others allow an OCP-only option. With the OCP-only option, dividends are paid as cash to the shareholder, but the shareholder may still make OCPs through the DRIP or DSP. For those who rely on dividend income (such as retirees), these can be attractive features.

If you do have a DRIP or DSP plan where these options exist, you need to keep an even more careful watch on the statements to be sure your investments are being accurately managed by the administrator.

Automatic Investment Plans

Many people who open DRIP and DSP accounts choose to invest automatically. We will talk more about the advantage of automatic investing in Chapter 8. If you invest automatically, you can set up an automatic electronic transfer between your bank account and your DRIP or DSP account. Each month, a sum is automatically transferred from the bank to the DRIP or DSP and then invested in additional shares of stock.

Even though it's automatic, you should get a statement when the transaction is complete. Check these statements carefully to be sure the DRIP or DSP administrator is accurately handling your automatic deposits. Errors can happen and it's best to fix them as early as possible.

As you set up the automatic withdrawal, try to time it a day or two before the company buys shares for their DRIP or DSP account holders. That way your money will get invested as quickly as possible in the stock you want.

Recordkeeping with Your Statements

In addition to checking your statements, you should also build a spreadsheet for each stock that you own. Over the life of the DRIP or DSP account, you will need to know how much cash you invested directly in the stock, as well as how much was reinvested for you from dividend payouts. You also should track any fees that you pay.

Build a spreadsheet that can help you keep track of the shares of stock you own and how much you paid for them. The spreadsheet should have at least six columns:

- Date of transaction
- Cash investments—dollar amount invested
- Cash investments—stock price paid
- Dividends—cash amount reinvested
- Dividends—stock price paid
- Number of shares held

By keeping this data you'll have everything you need to satisfy the IRS on one spreadsheet when you need to calculate the cost basis of your stock purchases. You will need to total any annual commissions and fees paid to buy these shares, so you may want to add a column to track those costs as well. If you can't prove what you paid for the stock, you could end up paying more capital gains taxes than necessary.

You should be able to find all the information you need for the spreadsheet on the statements you receive from your DRIP or DSP administrator. You should make it a habit to update the spreadsheet when you get the quarterly statement. That way you'll be certain all the transactions for the quarter have been added to the account. Compare the additions to those for which you have transaction statements to double check the information on your quarterly report.

Here's what the spreadsheet should look like:

Stock A—DRIP

Date of Investments	Cash Investments		Dividend Investments		Number of Shares Held
	Cash Invested	Stock Price	Dividend Reinvested	Stock Price	
Jan. 2009	$500	$50			10
Feb. 2009	$100	$51			11.9608
Mar. 2009	$100	$49	$14.95	$49	14.3067
April 2009	$100	$50			16.3067
May 2009	$100	$48			18.3900
June 2009	$100	$47	$22.98	$47	21.0066
July 2009	$100	$49			23.0474
Aug. 2009	$100	$50			25.0474
Sept. 2009	$100	$50	$31.31	$50	27.6736
Oct. 2009	$100	$51			29.6344
Nov. 2009	$100	$52			31.5575
Dec. 2009	$100	$53	$39.47		34.1890
2009 Total Cash and Dividend Investments	$1,600		$108.71		
Average Price Paid Per Share	$\frac{(\$1,600 + \$108.71)}{34.19 \text{ total shares}} = \$49.9784$ price per share				

In this sample chart for Stock A, I assumed a $500 initial investment with a $100 per month automatic investment. You can see that each month the stock price went up and down throughout the year.

At the end of the year the stock price was $53, but the average price paid per share was just $49.9784. That's because some shares were bought for as low as $47 and some for as high as $53. At $53 the total holdings of 34.1890 is worth $1,812.01. The investor only put in $1,600 cash and ended up with $212.01 more in total portfolio value. This $212 included $108.71 in reinvested dividends plus $103.30 in capital gains.

If you maintain this spreadsheet over the years, you'll have a total of the cash you invested out of pocket, as well as the cash that was reinvested for you as part of dividend reinvestments.

I did simplify the numbers to show you the basics. You will need to adjust them based on the statements you get from the account administrator.

For example, while I put the full amount of cash investments in each column, you may find that with a $100 investment there is a $2 or $5 processing fee, so your cash investment would only be $98 or $95. You should also track any commissions and fees that you paid. Those will also be needed to calculate your total cost for buying the shares of stock when you try to calculate your capital gains taxes. We talk more about this in Chapter 12.

You should find a summary on your year-end statement that will give you the total fees and commissions paid. If that is not the case, you may want to add a column to the spreadsheet that keeps a running total of all fees. Remember that these fees will be subtracted before the money is invested.

Now that you know what to look for in the statements, let's take a look at why automatic investing works so well for DRIP and DSP accounts.

The Least You Need to Know

- You will get statements for each transaction in your DRIP or DSP account. Always check them carefully for accuracy.

- You should get quarterly and annual financial statements for your DRIP and DSP accounts. Be certain that these statements include all your transactions.

- Keep your own spreadsheet to monitor your account cumulatively, so you can keep abreast of how well your investment is doing.

Chapter 8

Automatic Investing

In This Chapter

- How it works
- Understanding costs
- Avoid market timing
- Purchase options

Direct stock investing using DRIPs and DSPs works best when you make a long-term commitment to the companies you choose for your portfolio. Over the years you should make the decision to add money to your holdings. In addition, you should reinvest your dividends to keep building up your stock ownership.

Making regular monthly or quarterly investments automatically is the best way to see your dream of a sizeable stock portfolio materialize. In this chapter, we'll talk about why investing automatically works best and how to do it.

Why Automatic Investing Works

By deciding to have money taken out of your bank account automatically on a regular basis, you make a commitment to build a portfolio without having to remember to write a check. It's the easiest way to get started and it helps you to avoid making excuses for not investing one month. People tend to find reasons to skip or forget an investment if they actually have to write out a check each month.

You can set up an automatic electronic funds transfer (EFT) that will help you avoid the temptation of putting off an investment. Since it takes effort to cancel an EFT, you're more likely to just figure out a way to work around it. Of course, if an emergency comes up and you must stop investing automatically for a short time, do so. Don't skip paying credit card bills just so you can invest.

Direct Aids

Develop an investing plan and stick to it. People who continue to invest regularly and build a well-diversified portfolio tend to be the most successful investors. Although some are successful at day-trading and other trading schemes, these schemes only work if you have the time and the skills to trade full time. About 80 percent of people who try day-trading lose money.

But do try to budget things so you can make a commitment to set aside a certain amount each month. It doesn't have to be as high as $100 per month, since many DRIP and DSP plans allow additional investments for as little as $10 or $25 per month. But do watch your fees. If a company with which you want to open a DRIP or DSP account charges a lot for optional cash investments, you may want to set aside a certain amount of cash each month for investments in a special savings account at your own bank, and then buy stock in the DRIP or DSP less frequently to avoid excessive fees.

For example, suppose your DSP or DRIP charges $5 for each optional cash purchase. If you invest just $25 per month, that means 20 percent of your purchase will go toward fees. Only $20 of the $5 will go toward buying stock. To avoid this problem, set aside $25 per month in an investment savings account and buy stock when you have $100 or more to invest. That will lower your investment costs to just 5 percent.

If you do choose this method, you should still decide on an automatic investment plan and buy stock periodically, possibly every quarter or half year. You won't get the full benefits of dollar-cost averaging, but it will be better than paying excessive fees.

An even better choice would be to look for companies to add to your DRIP that don't charge a fee or charge less for optional cash investments. In Appendix C, where we focus on companies that offer DRIPs or DSPs, we include information about investing costs for each company. In Chapter 11, we talk about potential problems with DRIPs and DSPs, and excessive fees is one of the problems we discuss in that chapter.

Purchase Pitfalls

You can see that avoiding fees as much as possible will help you build your portfolio the fastest. If you choose a company that charges excessive fees, you may not find its DRIP or DSP beneficial. Consider buying stock through a discount broker if DSP or DRIP fees are high. We talk about this option in Chapter 10 on synthetic DRIPs.

The Advantage of Dollar-Cost Averaging

When you invest a set amount on a regular basis, you are using an investing strategy called dollar-cost averaging. When the price of a stock is up, you buy fewer shares of stock, but when the price of a stock is down you buy more shares of stock. Over time the average price you've paid for your stock will be less than what you would have paid if you tried to time the market and guess the best time to buy.

When using a dollar-cost averaging strategy ...

- You must invest a fixed amount on a regular basis, regardless of stock market fluctuations.

- You will end up buying more shares at a low price and fewer shares when the price is higher.

- You are not guaranteed a profit and it cannot protect you from a loss in the market, but over the long term, if you pick good companies, you will see growth in your portfolio.

- You must buy shares in both up and down markets in order for this strategy to work. Don't try to time the market.

Let's take a look at how this strategy might work over a few years. To give you an example, we'll use Company A and show regular purchases of $100 by quarter.

Quarterly Investment of $100	Stock Price	Number of Shares Bought	Total Shares in the Portfolio
Q1—2008	$10	10	10
Q2—2008	$11	9.0909	19.0909
Q3—2008	$9	11.1111	30.2020
Q4—2008	$8	12.5	42.7020
Q1—2009	$9	11.1111	53.8131
Q2—2009	$10	10	63.8131
Q3—2009	$12	8.3333	72.1464
Q4—2009	$15	6.6667	78.8131

As you can see from this chart, after two years of regular quarterly investments of $100, $800 was invested in Company A and 78.8131 shares were held at the end of the two-year period.

You can calculate the average share price by dividing $800 by the number of shares held:

$800 ÷ 78.8131 = $10.15—average price per share

Yet in this scenario, the buyer paid between $8 and $15 per share. Since the shares at the end of 2009 were selling for $15 per share, calculate the value of this investor's Company A stock holding by multiplying the number of shares held by the current stock price:

$15 × 78.8131 = $1,182.20—total stock value

You can see that in just two years, the total investment of $800 is worth $382.50 more, thanks to dollar-cost averaging. In a normal investment there would also be shares purchased with reinvested dividends. To keep calculations simple, we did not include dividend reinvestments here.

This strategy works so well because with this sample investment, 12.5 shares were bought when the stock was just $8 per share, but only 6.6667 shares were bought when the stock was $15.

Fees and Dollar-Cost Averaging

In developing this example we did not discuss the impact of fees on dollar-cost averaging. Fees will have a negative impact on the number of shares you purchase, but they won't change the benefits of dollar-cost averaging.

For example, suppose a company charged $3 per EFT. In that case, the amount used to buy shares each month would have been $97 rather than $100. In the first quarter, rather than buying 10 shares, you would only have been able to buy 9.7 shares.

That's why fees can be such a crucial factor when building a long-term portfolio. We talk more about the problem and what to do about it in Chapter 11.

Avoid Market Timing

You may be wondering why market timing wouldn't work better. Can't you just buy stock when the price is low and skip purchasing stock when the price is high? The problem with that strategy is that no one can successfully time the market consistently. Some are successful for a short period of time, but unless you have a crystal ball, market timing is impossible.

Hopefully the stock you choose will go up significantly over the years. But by waiting to buy stock only when it bottoms out, you could miss a lot of good buying opportunities.

Now, if you believe a stock price has been beaten down unnecessarily and you want to invest a bit extra during that period, you won't get hurt. This type of investing is called value investing. If you want to learn more about that, you can read *The Complete Idiot's Guide to Value Investing* (Alpha Books, 2009). But you could get hurt if you see a lot of excitement about the company in which you choose to invest and that excitement drives up the stock price. Buying extra shares at that time will be a mistake. The price has been driven high and likely will be driven higher than its true value by rumor and fall back down.

Remember the old adage, "Buy low and sell high." You always want to try to buy stock when the price is low and sell it when the price is high. Many investors make the mistake of getting into the market when it's up and then run from the market when it's down. What they end up doing is buying high and selling low. That's a great way to lose a lot of money.

Purchase Pitfalls

Don't get caught up in the hype of the marketplace. Keep to your steady investment plan and you'll build a long-term portfolio for your retirement or whatever investing goals you have.

How to Start Investing Automatically

You can invest automatically in several different ways. You can set up an EFT between the DRIP or DSP administrator and your bank. You can set up your online bill pay account to send out a check on a regular basis. Or you can send out the check yourself.

Electronic Funds Transfer

With most companies, investing automatically is just a matter of filling out a form telling the company's DRIP or DSP administrator how much you want to invest and how regularly you want to make that investment. You will have to attach a voided check. The company's stock administrator can then use the information to set up an EFT. Each month the company will take the set amount you instruct them to take out of your bank account. Many DRIP prospectuses and applications will use "ACH" to indicate that they accept electronic transfers. "ACH" is the abbreviation for "Automated Clearing House," which is the national network that coordinates electronic financial transfers between institutions.

If you do set up an EFT, be aware that it can sometimes take a few weeks or more to cancel that EFT, so be certain your budget can handle the amount you specify for a long period.

Emergencies do happen, and over the years you may occasionally need to send instructions to change that EFT. Call the DRIP or DSP administrator and ask how to temporarily or permanently stop an EFT. Most likely they will send you a form to fill out, or ask you to send a letter specifying the change in writing. When money is involved, every DRIP or DSP administrator will want a paper trail.

Purchase Pitfalls

Don't expect to be able to call and cancel an EFT withdrawal in a matter of days. You will likely need to wait several weeks or possibly a month or two to cancel an EFT, depending upon how a DRIP or DSP administrator handles the change.

Online Bill Pay

Another way to set up automatic investing is to set up your online bill pay to make a payment on a regular basis, whether it's weekly, monthly, or quarterly. You will maintain more control over the payment because it usually takes only seconds to change or cancel an online bill pay, as long as the payment is not already in processing.

Whether or not you choose this method will depend upon how much the fees are. Many DRIP and DSP administrators charge one fee for an EFT and a higher fee if you pay by check. You may find that your bank will use your bill pay instruction to send the money by EFT, or it may send the payment by check. Find out which method is used. If your bank can do an EFT, then you should be able to get the lowest fees, but if it sends a check, your cost of investing could go up dramatically. For example, some companies charge $5 per investment by check, but only $2 or $3 per investment by EFT. That may not sound like much, but it does add up over the years. Each time you invest,

it will be $2 or $3 more that won't go toward buying shares of stock.

Sending Checks

If you're not comfortable investing using an EFT
or online bill pay, you can choose to send checks
on a regular basis. This will be your most costly
option. Not only do you have to consider the costs
of your checks, your postage stamps, and your
envelopes, you also should expect to pay a higher
fee for the investment.

Many DRIP and DSP administrators do prefer to
work by EFT, and they make that clear by charging more for processing optional cash payments
made by check. Not every administrator does
charge more, so be sure to check the prospectus for
the companies you choose for your portfolio.

Purchase Pitfalls

Investing by sending checks regularly
does give you the most control,
but it also makes it the easiest to skip a
payment. Strongly consider using EFT or
automatic online bill pay to reduce the
temptation of skipping a payment.

If you do decide to send checks, then write out the
envelopes at the beginning of each year. You'll need
4 envelopes if you're sending the additional investments in quarterly and you'll need 12 envelopes

if you're sending the investments in monthly. Put these envelopes where you pay your bills so you don't forget to send the investment.

Now that we've looked at how to invest automatically, let's take a closer look at how you use direct stock investing to build your retirement savings through IRAs.

The Least You Need to Know

- Automatic investing ensures that you won't forget or find excuses to avoid making investments regularly.
- With automatic investing, you take advantage of an investing method that works—dollar-cost averaging.
- You can invest automatically using three different methods: EFT, online bill pay, or sending checks.

Direct Stock Investing Using IRAs

In This Chapter

- Investing options
- Self-administering your IRA
- DRIP-sponsored IRAs
- Synthetic DRIPs and IRAs

As a long-term investing tool, DRIPs or DSPs can be an excellent option for building your retirement portfolio, tax-free or tax-deferred, with very low administrative costs.

In this chapter, we'll look at how you can use direct stock investing to build your retirement portfolio, and focus on some of the best companies with which you can open an Individual Retirement Account (IRA) custodian account.

How to Invest Using an IRA

You will find it challenging to find just the right companies with which to open your DRIP or

DSP IRA. You won't be able to use just any stock. You'll need to commit to finding companies whose account administrators are willing to go the extra mile to manage a DRIP or DSP within an IRA—or you'll need to find an *independent IRA custodian*.

def•i•ni•tion

> An **independent IRA custodian** does not offer affiliated investment products and allows you to direct your retirement funds to be invested in any qualified investment that meets your requirements.

If you are committed to the idea of building an IRA through DRIPs or DSPs, you will find at least three options available:

- Self-administered IRAs
- DRIP- or DSP-sponsored IRAs
- Reinvesting dividends in brokerage IRAs

Using DRIPs and DSPs in Self-Administered IRAs

The option that will likely give you the most control and flexibility is to set up a self-administered IRA through a broker or other IRA administrator, who can assist you with investing using DRIPs and DSPs.

Because an IRA requires a trustee, such as a bank, mutual fund company, or brokerage firm, you must find a custodian for your account that will permit the reinvestment of dividends on securities that you hold directly. If your broker won't do it—and many won't because they won't earn any commissions on the IRA—you might need to manage your IRA through an independent IRA custodian.

These self-directed IRAs differ from the typical retirement accounts offered by banks or brokerage firms because they allow you to hold nontraditional assets such as limited partnerships, limited liability companies, direct participation programs, real property, deeds of trust for mortgages, and of course, DRIPs and DSPs.

A self-directed IRA requires you to make investment decisions on behalf of your retirement plan, but you must place those funds with a qualified trustee—an independent IRA custodian. You can't just put the funds in a bank account and call it an IRA. Usually the trustee or custodian maintains the assets and all transaction records, files reports for the IRS, issues statements, and helps you with the sometimes convoluted rules and regulations pertaining to IRS administration.

But remember, the trustee is not responsible and will not guarantee that the investments you choose do meet the rules and regulations of the IRS. So in order to be sure you comply with all rules and regulations, check with a tax attorney or accountant to be sure your plans meet IRS stipulations for IRAs. If not, you could end up paying additional taxes and penalties.

The custodian's job is to follow the directions of the account holder as a *nondiscretionary trustee*. They have no obligation to make sure you are following IRS rules.

def•i•ni•tion

> A **nondiscretionary trustee** is a trustee who has no discretion or personal decision-making power in your investment choices.

You can choose to build your portfolio in two types of IRAs—a traditional IRA that is tax-deductible, or a Roth IRA that is not tax-deductible. To use a tax-deductible IRA, you cannot also participate in an employer-sponsored retirement plan, such as a 401(k) or pension plan. Contributions to your tax-deductible IRA can be deducted when you file your taxes. But you will pay taxes when you start to take the money out of the IRA during retirement.

If you choose to use a Roth IRA, you can't deduct your contributions to that IRA, but as you take your money out in retirement, you won't have to pay taxes on it. Another big advantage of the Roth IRA is that you don't have to start taking the money out of the IRA at any time, whereas with a traditional IRA you must start withdrawing funds at the age of 70½ or else pay penalties.

Both IRAs limit the amount you can invest each year. In 2009 the annual limit was $5,000. If you are over 50, you are allowed catch-up contributions and can put in another $1,000 for a total of $6,000.

The amount that you are allowed to put into an IRA will go up periodically, based on inflation, in increments of $500, so follow news reports on IRAs to know when those limits are raised.

There are limits on who can invest using a tax-free Roth IRA. A couple who wants to invest with a Roth IRA must have a modified adjusted gross income (MAGI) below $166,000. If your MAGI is between $166,000 and $176,000, you may be able to contribute some money to an IRA, but that ability phases out gradually until your MAGI tops $176,000. If your income is close to the phase-out level, talk with your accountant before opening a Roth IRA. That phase-out range is also adjusted yearly for inflation, so watch news reports to know what the amount is each year.

For single individuals, the Roth IRA phase-out limit is lower: $105,000 to $120,000 for 2009. So if your income is above $120,000, you cannot use a Roth IRA.

If you can't qualify for a traditional tax-deductible IRA or a Roth IRA, you still may be able to use a non-tax-deductible IRA. Your contributions won't be tax-deductible and you will have to pay taxes when you take your money out as well, but at least you can grow your retirement portfolio tax-deferred. Tax-deferred means you won't have to pay taxes on dividends and capital gains until you start to take the money out of your IRA. At that time you'll pay tax only on the money you take out each year, based on your current income tax rate.

Independent IRA Custodians

As you research independent IRA custodians, you'll find these firms typically charge an initial set-up fee of about $50 and an annual administrative charge—usually ½ or 1 percent of your account—or charge you a set amount on a flat-rate fee basis. Flat-rate fees can range from $60 to $1,100 or more depending on the company you choose and the size of your assets.

Pick an independent IRA custodian carefully and be sure to research fees before opening an account. A fee that is just ½ or 1 percent may sound low when you're just starting to build your IRA, but will be a lot more when your IRA has grown to $100,000 or more. For that reason, flat-fee custodians are usually better to work with over the long term.

Three major independent IRA custodian companies that you can work with include Pensco Trust Company, Sunwest Trust, and IRA Services.

Pensco Trust Company

Pensco Trust Company's (www.penscotrust.com) sole business since 1989 has been supporting self-directed IRAs. Pensco is chartered in New Hampshire and focuses on being the country's preferred special-asset custodian for self-directed IRAs.

The company's custodian services focus on the administration and custody of IRAs invested in

nontraded assets, such as those within self-directed
real estate IRAs, self-directed private placement
IRAs, self-directed Roth IRAs, SEP IRAs, and
Solo(k)s. You can call for more information about
Pensco's services at 1-866-818-4472.

Sunwest Trust

Sunwest Trust (www.sunwesttrust.com) offers you
the opportunity to self-direct your IRA with a wide
variety of retirement plans, including Roth IRAs,
spousal and traditional IRAs, SEPs, and SIMPLEs.
Sunwest Trust acts as custodian for your retirement account while allowing you to direct the
investments within your account.

In addition to DRIPs or DSPs, Sunwest Trust
permits you to invest in real estate, mortgages,
real estate contracts, publicly traded stocks, bonds,
mutual funds, private limited partnerships, private
stock offerings, private limited liability companies,
and secured and unsecured notes. You can call
Sunwest Trust for more information at 1-800-642-
7167.

IRA Services

IRA Services (www.iraservices.com) provides
retirement services and administers over 19,000
retirement accounts. Through IRA services you
can choose a wide variety of standard and nonstandard investments, including limited partnerships,
limited liability companies, promissory notes
(secured and unsecured), real estate investment
trusts, real estate land and income properties,

private placements, mutual funds, and stock in public and private companies.

IRA Services works with Fremont Bank to provide a complete self-directed IRA custodial service for investors. Fremont Bank provides an FDIC-insured savings account that will earn you interest until you make your investment. You can call IRS Services at 650-593-2221.

DRIP- and DSP-Sponsored IRAs

You may not need to find an independent IRA custodian. Some companies offer DRIP-sponsored IRAs. You may even find Education IRAs and Roth IRA options. Read the prospectus of the company to find out if they have an IRA option.

Here are some companies that do allow you to open IRAs using their DRIP programs:

- American Electric Power Co.
- Ameritech
- Atmos Energy
- Connecticut Water
- Exxon-Mobil
- Ford Motor
- GTE
- McDonald's
- Morton International
- Sears
- Wal-Mart

You will find that these companies charge an annual fee that ranges from $35 to $50 for maintaining your IRA, but that will probably be less than the amount you'll pay an independent IRA custodian. But remember, you need to pay that fee to each company that will open an IRA for you and serve as custodian.

Brokerage DRIPs

You can also open your IRA through a brokerage company and invest your IRA funds using a brokerage DRIP. Many brokerage firms advertise free dividend reinvestment services for account holders. These plans are often known as "synthetic DRIPs." We take a closer look at synthetic DRIPs in Chapter 10.

The big difference between a brokerage DRIP and a company-sponsored DRIP is that company DRIPs allow account holders to purchase additional shares at little or no commission. On the other hand, few brokers are willing to waive their commissions for account holders. They may be willing to reinvest dividends for you at no cost, but you'll have to pay a commission if you want to buy more shares.

Another major disadvantage of synthetic DRIPs is that brokers will only reinvest dividends in purchases of whole shares, not fractional shares. As a small investor, you won't have the advantage of seeing the number of shares grow as rapidly over time until you own hundreds or thousands of shares.

Remember, when you are able to buy fractional shares, they can earn dividends as well, rather than sitting in a cash account earning very little interest. Your stock holdings will grow faster when you can buy fractional shares.

Now that you understand the options you have for building an IRA using DRIPs or DSPs, we'll take a closer look at the option of working with a traditional broker using a synthetic DRIP or DSP account.

The Least You Need to Know

- There are three methods for investing using DRIPs or DSPs: self-administered IRAs, DRIP-sponsored IRAs, and reinvesting dividends in brokerage IRAs.

- If you want to build your own IRA with DRIPs or DSPs, you need to use an independent IRA custodian.

- In some cases you can avoid working with an independent custodian if the company through which you set up your DRIP or DSP offers IRA custodian services.

- You can also open an IRA through a brokerage firm that offers free reinvestment of dividends and can serve as your IRA custodian.

Chapter 10

Synthetic DRIPs

In This Chapter

- Broker DRIPs
- Synthetic DRIP advantages
- Portfolio management
- Best synthetic DRIP broker

You can arrange to have your dividends reinvested through a broker at no cost. Many brokers do offer that service. But this is not a real DRIP. It's known as a synthetic DRIP. In this chapter, we explore the pros and cons of synthetic DRIPs and how they may enable you to better manage your portfolio.

Setting Up a Broker DRIP

Before you buy your first share of stock with any broker, ask about the broker's policy on reinvesting dividends. Many do allow their customers to reinvest dividends at no cost. It's a service they provide.

If a broker you are considering responds that they do charge commissions on dividend reinvestment, and you want to start using DRIP investment strategies, don't open the account. So many brokers do not charge for dividend reinvestment that you can easily take your business elsewhere, and we recommend that you do just that if you want to be a DRIP investor.

Reinvesting your dividends at no cost is a service provided by brokers called a "synthetic DRIP." It's not the real thing, but if the company you choose doesn't have a DRIP, a synthetic DRIP may be your best option.

The biggest benefit of a synthetic DRIP is that you can buy shares of stock in a company that doesn't have a DRIP and still drip your stocks. A broker that offers this service allows you to drip virtually every blue-chip company on the U.S. stock exchanges.

Although synthetic DRIPs have expanded the number of drippable companies available to you, they do have two key drawbacks:

- Most brokerage firms do not allow you to buy fractional shares. Only full shares will be purchased and the remainder of any dividend will be deposited as cash in your trading account. A few do allow fractional share purchases including Schwab, E*Trade, and TD Ameritrade, as well as brokerage accounts at Fidelity and Vanguard, but you won't be able to transfer these fractional shares into or out of the account.

- You won't be able to buy new shares for a minimal fee. If you want to buy additional shares, you have to pay the regular commission fees of your broker.

Why should it matter whether or not you can buy fractional shares? Suppose Company A pays a $15 quarterly dividend and the current share price is $10 per share. If you had a real DRIP, you would be able to purchase 1.5 shares. But the company managing your synthetic DRIP will only let you buy one and put the $5 in your trading account, most likely a money market account. Each time you get dividends, your broker will buy the number of whole shares your dividend can afford and put the rest in your money market account, where the money sits until your account has enough money to buy another whole share. (As mentioned previously, a few brokers will let you buy fractional shares but you won't be able to transfer these shares into or out of an account.)

But suppose you had $5 from the first quarter and $5 from the second quarter and you're now ready to buy a share at $10. At that point you would also have to pay a brokerage commission to purchase the additional share. Suppose that commission is $9. You certainly aren't going to want to spend $9 to buy one share of stock for $10, so you'll probably wait until you have even more cash. Unless you put in a lot of additional cash, you likely won't buy additional shares for many years but instead let that cash build up.

Direct Aids

The biggest advantage of a real DRIP opened directly with a company is that you can build fractional shares every quarter. These fractional shares would earn even more dividends, and long term, you would have a much larger portfolio.

Brokerage fees may or may not be a big issue. It will depend upon the fees charged by the companies with which you have your DRIPs. For example, suppose your DRIP charges you $5 for additional cash purchases. Your plan is to invest $50 per month. While a DRIP will allow you to buy fractional shares, during a quarter you would invest $150 and pay $15 in fees ($5 for each of the three months of investments). If instead you work with a discount broker that allows you to buy shares at $9 per transaction or less, which many discount brokers do, you could deposit $50 per month in a money market account with the broker and then buy $150 worth of shares on a quarterly basis for a fee of just $9.

Over time you would save a significant amount of money in fees. In just one year you would have paid $60 (12 × $5) to the account administrator for the company with which you have your DRIP. But if you worked with a broker using a synthetic DRIP, your quarterly purchases would have cost you just $36 (4 × $9).

So when deciding whether to use a real or synthetic DRIP, consider the fees you will pay for both and pick the option that will cost you the least. Remember, fees are taken out before you buy the stock, so they essentially represent money never invested.

Advantages of a Synthetic DRIP

While synthetic DRIPs can delay the building of a portfolio in a specific stock, they do have benefits:

- They allow you to determine the stocks into which you want to invest your extra cash from dividends. You could use the cash to buy stock in a company that didn't pay you the dividends.

- They allow you to manage a portfolio of a number of stocks from one brokerage account.

- They provide free access to the analyst reports offered by the brokerage house.

- They provide you with consolidated monthly statements.

Let's take a closer look at what these advantages mean to you as a synthetic DRIP investor.

Pick Stocks for Investment

Since the broker may only allow you to buy whole shares and not fractional shares with a synthetic DRIP, the extra cash dividends you get will be automatically deposited into your trading account. Each quarter all the extra cash you can't use to buy fractional shares will be deposited in that money market account. This extra cash from dividends you earn will be from all the stocks you own. Your additional monthly automatic investments will go into that account until you specify the stock you want to buy.

This could actually be an advantage for some investment strategies. You will then be able to choose how to "reinvest" your dividends and choose the security in which you want to buy more shares. This strategy (which is a form of "value cost averaging") works whether or not your broker offers fractional share reinvestment (or dividend reinvestment at all!). In other words, keeping your cash dividends in your brokerage account until you decide how you want to invest them can be a valid strategy and not just a workaround.

Also, your fractional shares won't add up very quickly at all. For example, for a typical $20 stock, the most you could have left over from a dividend that wouldn't buy a full share is $19.99. While it's true that the reinvestment of small dividends over many years can contribute a lot to a portfolio's total return, the principle of "reinvesting all earnings" is really key, whether you reinvest the dividends in the same stock or another stock—just don't withdraw the dividends paid by your stocks and spend them!

With the money market account, you get to choose which stocks you want to purchase. Suppose you own IBM and Johnson & Johnson. Both companies paid dividends. Since your broker provides you with a synthetic DRIP, some of those dividends were used to buy additional shares, but not all the cash could be used because the broker does not allow you to purchase fractional shares. The cash that would have been used to buy fractional shares in a real DRIP were deposited as cash in your money market account. You can then use that cash to buy whatever stock you want. You could decide you want to diversify and add another stock or you could decide you want to use the cash from both IBM and Johnson & Johnson to buy additional shares of just Johnson & Johnson.

Synthetic DRIPs give you the flexibility to decide how to reinvest those dividends, but that benefit could also become a problem if you're not disciplined and don't reinvest your dividends. Using synthetic DRIPs do require you to be even more disciplined about investing regularly.

Portfolio Management

Managing a portfolio of real DRIPs requires a lot of recordkeeping on your part (we talked about the records you need to keep in Chapter 7). You also need to set up a spreadsheet to keep track of your portfolio's *asset allocation*.

def•i•ni•tion

> **Asset allocation** is the process of dividing investments among different kinds of assets, such as stocks, bonds, real estate, and cash, to minimize risk and meet your long-term goals.

You probably are aware that stock markets always go up and down. Different stocks do better in different economic environments. Within the allocation you've set aside for stocks, you want to build a diversified portfolio over a cross-section of industries. This relates to the old adage of "don't put all your eggs in one basket." You can diversify by buying stocks in different industries. That way if one industry is hit particularly hard in a given cycle, you'll hold stocks in other industries that are not as hard hit.

Also it's good to buy stocks in cyclical or seasonal industries as well as in companies that do well year round. For example, food industry stocks tend to do well year round, while toy company stocks do best during particular sales seasons.

When we are in the initial recovery period after an economic downturn, basic industry stocks and energy stocks tend to take the early lead. After we've gotten into full recovery, you can expect the safest stocks to be companies that offer the essentials of life, such as food and health care. As we move into the next recession, everyone will need these basic staples of life.

In the early stages of a recession, banks and insurance company stocks tend to do the best. During a full recession, customers look for safety. Consumer spending is slow and interest rates drop. So the types of stocks that tend to take the lead are technology stocks and cyclical stocks.

By building a portfolio with a good representation of a variety of industries, you can ride out many economic storms with a well-balanced portfolio. You also need to hold bonds and cash to minimize the risk to your portfolio. The amount of money you hold in each asset will depend upon your risk tolerance.

Another key factor in building a portfolio is the amount of time you have before you'll need the money. If you'll need the money in about two to three years, you shouldn't invest in the stock market at all. Markets go up and down and you don't want to be stuck needing cash when the stock market is down—you'll be forced to sell stock at a loss. Generally if you think you will need the money in the next two years, it's best to keep it in cash. Money that you need in three to five years should be invested in bonds. Only money that you know you won't need for at least five years should be invested in stocks. That way you'll have the time to wait out a downturn in the stock market.

If you know you won't need the money for at least 10 years and you can tolerate a greater degree of risk, you can consider a portfolio of 80 percent stocks and 20 percent cash or bonds. However, many people find this level of investment too risky.

A good mix for many people is a combination of 50 percent stocks and 50 percent bonds and/or cash. The key is that you are able to sleep at night and not worry about what the market is doing every day.

The crash of 2008–2009 showed that even a 50/50 portfolio was too risky, because both bonds and stocks were hard hit. Usually just one or the other is hard hit, and by balancing your portfolio between the two, you always hold something with a gain that can be sold. Unfortunately, both markets were hit at the same time in this crash, and many retirees lost 40 or 50 percent of their retirement portfolio and income.

No, there are no guarantees when you invest your money in stocks and bonds. But socking it away under your mattress or putting it in a low interest-earning bank account comes with risks, too. The key risk you face with this type of investing is the risk that your portfolio will be so low earning that you'll lose money simply to inflation.

So your best bet is to carefully manage your portfolio for risk, but don't take on too much or too little risk. What is too much or too little risk? Each person needs to decide the comfortable risk levels for himself or herself. Like most of life, there are no absolutes; you just have to find your own balance. But the general test is that if you're lying awake each night worrying about your portfolio, you've taken on too much risk.

Analyst Reports

You should always do your own research about the companies you choose for your portfolio, but having access to a number of analysts for each stock you are considering can be very helpful. When you have an account with an discount broker, you'll get free access to all the analyst reports the broker offers.

This can be a huge benefit over trying to find the research on your own. You can certainly go to your local library and use its reports from Standard & Poor's or Value Line. You can research stocks online at many different financial websites. But the detailed reports you can get from a broker are usually not available for free online unless you have a brokerage account.

Over the long term, many investors will own both real DRIPs and other stocks through a broker. Not all companies offer DRIPs or DSPs, so you will have to buy some stocks through a broker. As long as you have an open account with a broker, you will have access to all their research.

Consolidated Monthly Statements

For people managing many different stocks in their portfolio, a consolidated monthly statement can be a big benefit of synthetic DRIPs. For example, suppose you own real DRIPs in 10 different companies. You would get transaction statements and quarterly statements from each of these companies.

That means at least 10 statements every three months. With a synthetic DRIP, you would only have to sort through one statement every three months. That consolidation of information does make managing a synthetic DRIP easier than real DRIPs.

The Best Synthetic DRIP Broker

While many brokers do offer synthetic DRIPs, one broker stands out in the crowd—ShareBuilder (www.sharebuilder.com). This broker focuses on offering services to people who want to invest through DRIPs and DSPs.

ShareBuilder allows you to invest on a regularly scheduled basis with predetermined dollar amounts in more than 7,000 stocks and *exchange-traded funds* (*ETFs*). You can even purchase partial shares through ShareBuilder.

def•i•ni•tion

> Exchange-traded funds (ETFs) track an index, but can be traded like a stock. They are a basket of stocks that can be traded throughout the day.

When you set up an account with ShareBuilder, you can designate an automatic purchase based on a dollar amount you specify. ShareBuilder will invest that dollar amount for you and buy partial shares of stock, letting you accumulate positions over time. Each week ShareBuilder collects the orders their investors have specified and purchases shares in a large lump. This reduces the cost of purchasing additional shares in their customers' synthetic DRIPs.

Since you can choose the dollar amount you want to invest rather than the number of shares you want to buy, you will usually be buying shares in fractional amounts. This gives you the best of both worlds: you can invest a small amount monthly, buy fractional shares, and do all this at a fee that is lower than most other brokers. Few DRIPs and DSPs allow you to buy shares without paying a fee, but ShareBuilder's fees are close to those of real DRIPs and DSPs, and in some cases lower.

Suppose you want to invest $100 per month and the stock price for the company you want to buy is $60. Each month you would purchase 1.6667 shares. Since ShareBuilder is pooling the purchases, the actual fee for that purchase will be much less than it would be with a standard online broker.

You can set up to buy stocks weekly, biweekly, or monthly. The amount you'll pay for each stock purchase will depend upon the program you choose for your portfolio. With ShareBuilder's Basic program, you would pay $4 for each transaction. But for more active investors, they offer a Standard program that costs $12 per month and includes six investments each month. Additional investments are $2 each. For even larger investors with bigger portfolios, ShareBuilder offers an Advantage account for $20 per month with 20 investments included. Additional investments in this account cost $1 each.

Once your DRIP or DSP portfolio reaches at least six different companies, you may want to consider ShareBuilder if you are making and paying the fees for monthly cash investments in your individual DRIP and DSP accounts. Most DRIP and DSP administrators charge at least $2 to process optional cash investments. That matches the cost of ShareBuilder. If your DRIP or DSP administrator charges more, then ShareBuilder might make sense for you even before your portfolio is up to six different stocks.

Now that you understand how synthetic DRIPs work and have reviewed the pros and cons of synthetic DRIPs, let's take a look at the potential problems with DRIP and DSP investing.

The Least You Need to Know

- Before opening a brokerage account, be sure your broker allows dividend reinvestment for free.

- You can more easily diversify your holdings with a synthetic DRIP.

- Portfolio management can be a bit easier with a synthetic DRIP because you'll get consolidated statements rather than individual statements for each stock you hold.

- ShareBuilder is designed for synthetic DRIPs and offers you services for reinvestment of dividends and new cash purchases at a cost lower than other brokers.

Direct Stock Purchase Potential Problems

In This Chapter

- Purchase limitations
- Fewer stock choices
- Fees can be a drag
- Limit on investment amounts

Direct stock investing can be a great way to build a stock portfolio without having to pay brokerage commissions, but you have to work around some potential problems. Just be aware of these purchase pitfalls and plan your portfolio management strategies to avoid any problems. In this chapter, we explore the potential problems and talk about possible solutions.

Can't Set Your Purchase Targets

You won't be able to set a purchase price or even a purchase date for new shares of stock. Most DRIPs and DSPs have preset purchase and sell dates, so the company will buy and sell stocks for you based on these preset dates.

With this mind, don't plan to watch stock prices and be able to act on those prices if you choose to invest through DRIPs and DSPs. You won't be able to see a stock drop on Tuesday and wire cash to the DRIP or DSP administrator and order them to buy the stock in the same day. You also can't be sure you'll get the stock price you want. While you can do that with a limit order through a broker, there are no price controls with direct stock investing.

Each plan sets its own investment schedule to minimize transaction costs. Most plans set a date on a monthly or weekly basis on which the DRIP or DSP administrator buys or sells stocks for all plan participants. Some plans do buy and sell stocks daily.

Unless you are a technical trader, this shouldn't be a big problem for you. Your goal should be to build long-term wealth with DRIPs and DSPs, so a difference of a few cents on the day of purchase shouldn't be a major hindrance to your long-term plans.

Purchase Pitfalls

Don't choose to invest through DRIPs or DSPs if you are a stock speculator who likes to act on technical signs. You will be disappointed and quickly close your accounts.

Most of the stocks that pay dividends and offer DRIPs do not see wild daily swings in their market price. If you want some control over the price you pay for a stock, get to know a plan's investment dates. You'll find them in the plan's prospectus.

When you see the price of a stock near where you want to purchase that stock, be sure to send your check or arrange for an electronic funds transfer at least two to three days before that actual purchase date. For example, if the DRIP through which you invest buys and sells stock on the 15th of every month, be sure your money to purchase new shares of stock is in the hands of the DRIP or DSP administrator by the 12th or 13th.

By timing your purchases based on the DRIP or DSP administrator's schedule, you'll get the stock at a price near to the one you want, but there are no guarantees about the final stock price. You can get close, but you can't pick a price and place an order based on your ideal purchase price.

Know your plan's buy and sell restrictions when you decide to open a DRIP or DSP and keep track of any changes. That way you can plan your purchases around those restrictions. If you are an automatic investor, this issue won't affect you at all. Your weekly, monthly, or quarterly investment will be invested on the next transaction date. So don't worry about the transaction date and price limitations.

Limited Choices of Stocks

You can't open a DRIP or DSP with every stock on the exchange. About 1,600 companies offer a DRIP or DSP. We focus on some of them in Appendix C.

In order to open a direct stock investing account, the company must offer the option. But you can always set up a synthetic DRIP and have your dividends reinvested through most online discount brokers. We talked about synthetic DRIPs and how they work in Chapter 10.

Most of the companies that don't offer DRIPs or DSPs are smaller, and many of them don't pay dividends, so this should not be a major problem for you. You can still find a broad selection of industries represented in the DRIPs and DSPs that are offered. Most of the companies will be large, well-respected, blue-chip companies. So while your choices might be limited, in many industries it's the cream of the crop that offer DRIPs and DSPs.

Direct Aids

Just because you are investing by DRIPs and DSPs doesn't mean you are locked into only companies that offer them. You can open an account with an online discount broker to purchase shares in companies that don't offer a DRIP or DSP.

Buying small companies that don't offer DRIPs and DSPs can be a good way to diversify your portfolio in large and small companies. So as you have more money to invest to build your portfolio, you may want to buy stock in smaller companies that don't offer DRIPs and DSPs.

Watch Those Fees

Fees seem to be going up each year. As we were developing the list for Appendix C, we did see a number of companies that charge $5 or $6 plus a purchase charge per share. That purchase charge per share was usually 10¢ or less.

If you're investing just $10 per month and pay a fee of $5 for that investment, half your money goes toward fees rather than shares of stocks. So make sure you understand the fees being charged. Fees can be a huge drag on building a long-term portfolio.

If you do want to invest automatically in companies with hefty fees, you may want to consider a synthetic broker like ShareBuilder. We talk more about those portfolio-building options in Chapter 10.

Even if you are investing $100 and have to pay $5 or more in fees, you're still paying too much. That represents a 5 percent drag on your investment. So if you plan to invest $100 monthly, you could lower your investment costs in a DRIP that charges $5 per transaction by holding your monthly investments and sending them in quarterly. You'll still pay $5 for a transaction, but you'll pay that on a $300 investment, so that the transaction cost is just 1.7 percent. You probably won't be able to get your transaction fees any lower than that with an online broker. A good rule of thumb is to keep your transaction costs below 2 percent, and as close to 1 percent (or below) as possible.

Luckily you can still find a lot of companies that continue to offer their DRIPs and DSPs with no fees or fees of just $2 or $3 per transaction. As you pick companies, always track the fees you will pay. For example, suppose you want to buy stock from a public utility company. They usually pay sizeable dividends. If you find two that you like and one offers you the option to make additional cash investments with no transaction fees and the second charges you $3 per transaction, choose the one with the lower fees. Three dollars per transaction might not sound like a lot, but over the years it will add up.

Each time you pay a transaction fee, that's money that doesn't go toward buying shares of stock, which means you won't get the dividends on those lost shares either. Over the long term it will be a drag on your investment gains. That doesn't mean you shouldn't consider shares if the transaction fees are too high. If it's a company you really want to own, then by all means you should add it to your portfolio. Do an analysis of how you plan to buy your shares of stock and calculate how much you would pay in fees using various scenarios.

Direct Aids

If you want to buy shares of a company that charges high transaction fees, you may want to consider buying shares through an online broker or by using a synthetic DRIP.

For example, suppose you plan to invest $100 per month automatically. The company you've chosen charges $5 per transaction. With monthly transactions you would pay $60 per year. If you decide instead to put $100 per month in a money market account with a broker and buy shares four times a year at a price point you choose, you would then pay just $36 per year ($9 per transaction times 4 transactions). You can easily find an online broker that will offer you transaction fees at $9 per transaction.

If you choose to use an online broker rather than open a DRIP or DSP, be certain that broker offers you the capability of reinvesting your dividends at no cost. Most brokers do, but the disadvantage is that brokers will only buy whole shares, not fractional shares. So you will have to wait until you get enough dividends to buy at least one share.

Since the ability to buy fractional shares is a big advantage of DRIPs and DSPs, you could decide to invest $300 quarterly rather than $100 monthly in your DRIP. Then you would pay just $20 per year for 4 transactions at $5 rather than $60 for 12 transactions at $5.

Another twist in DRIP and DSP fees is that some companies charge more when you send a check than when you make purchases by electronic funds transfer (EFT). We've seen charges of $5 for cash sent by check and as low as $2 from the same company for automatic investments sent by EFT. So be sure you know all your investment options and the fees for those options.

Develop an investing strategy that will maximize the amount of money that will be used to buy shares of stock and minimize the amount you'll pay in transaction fees. That way you won't waste your money on fees and most of it will go toward building your portfolio.

Investment Limits

You can't invest an unlimited dollar amount when you buy stock through a DRIP or DSP plan. Most companies limit the amount you can invest with each transaction, as well as the number of transactions you can make per year. Others limit the total amount you can invest for the year.

You probably will never hit the maximum investment limits if you are a small investor. For most companies the investment limit is usually something like $10,000 or more per month. Many companies allow you to buy as much as $350,000 to $500,000 per year. If you really do have that much money to invest commission-free, you really can't complain that the company sets limits.

The minimum investment limits, however, may pose a problem with some DRIP and DSP plans. Some companies require a purchase of at least $100, but many allow purchases of at least $10 per month. As long as you have at least $10 per month to invest, you should have a good selection of companies from which to choose.

Direct Aids

As you choose your companies, be sure to check their minimum purchase limits. If those limits are higher than what you can afford, look at other companies. Otherwise you'll just keep missing investment opportunities as you try to set aside the required minimum.

The key to all of this is that you find the right DRIPs and DSPs that will allow you to invest automatically without excuses. The most important thing is that you invest and save regularly.

If you really do want a company whose minimum investment amount is higher than your budget, consider a synthetic DRIP like ShareBuilder. ShareBuilder will allow you to build your portfolio with fractional shares and you will be able to get around the minimums for companies that set very high minimums. We talk more about how this works in Chapter 10.

Keep Those Records

One of the things almost everyone hates is to keep detailed records and a good filing system. When you decide to invest through DRIPs and DSPs, it's crucial that you develop good recordkeeping habits.

You must track each of your small monthly investments and dividend reinvestments. These small amounts will add up to be the cost basis of your investment. If you can't prove how much you paid to buy the stock, you could end up paying more in capital gains taxes than you should when you sell the stock.

Purchase Pitfalls

Don't throw away transaction paperwork or year-end statements. You'll need those when it comes time to sell the stock so you can prove how much you paid for the shares you own.

You should get a handle on recordkeeping as soon as you open your first DRIP or DSP account. Start a file for that account with the first paperwork you get from the DRIP or DSP, which should be your prospectus and a copy of your account application.

As you get confirmations of transactions, add those to the file. Also keep your quarterly reports, which should summarize all activity for each quarter. Your year-end statements will likely be your most critical documents, because they should summarize the total number of shares and the total dollar amount invested for that year.

The process for tracking DRIP and DSP investments is not difficult, just time consuming. The biggest problems will come when you decide to sell shares of stock. You will have to sort out your purchase prices for the shares of stock you own.

You can simplify this process a bit by using a spreadsheet to track all purchases, both additional cash purchases and dividend reinvestments. We talk more about the type of spreadsheets you can set up in Chapter 7.

Yes, extensive recordkeeping for a DRIP can be a pain in the neck, but the advantages that you get from dollar-cost averaging (see Chapter 8) far outweigh the disadvantages. Just start your files immediately upon your first purchase and keep them going. That way you'll be ready for the tax man and minimize the taxes you'll have to pay when you sell the stock.

In the next chapter, we'll review the key tax laws that have an impact on direct stock investing.

The Least You Need to Know

- You can't choose your buy and sell points. Companies have specific days each week or month on which they carry out transactions for all their DRIP or DSP participants.

- You can't invest in every stock using DRIPs or DSPs. About 1,600 companies offer you the option.

- Watch out for fees because they will be a drag on your investment. You can invest less frequently or choose to use a synthetic DRIP to avoid paying fees to companies that set them too high.

- You may find there are limits to how much you can invest. Most small investors are not affected by the maximum limits, but the minimum limits may be a deterrent. Be sure to check those limits before you open a DRIP or DSP account.

Chapter 12

Direct Stock Investing and Taxes

In This Chapter

- Taxable items
- Reporting differences
- Calculating capital gains
- Tax strategies

Investing through DRIPs and DSPs can complicate your taxes. If you've invested using mutual funds, you will find some similarities in what you must report to the IRS each year and what records you must keep to report the cost basis of your investments. If you have not done this kind of reporting before, you'll need to start developing new record-keeping habits.

In this chapter, we explore the nitty-gritty of the tax rules as they apply to DRIPs and DSPs. Then we look at the differences in how DRIP companies handle transactions and how they can affect your taxes. Finally, we discuss some additional tax strategies to consider when investing using DRIPs and DSPs.

What's Taxable

Most DRIP dividends that are paid on shares of stocks are considered qualifying dividends, so they are taxable at a rate of 10 percent for low-income individuals and 15 percent for others on your income tax return. If they are nonqualifying dividends, they will be taxed at the same rate as your ordinary income. Those are the tax rates at least through 2011 under current tax law. You should verify your tax rates with your tax advisor.

You must pay these taxes whether you reinvest the dividends or received them in cash. You must pay taxes on all dividends, reinvested or not, in the year in which you received the dividends. So if you are reinvesting your dividends, even though you didn't get cash, you still need to pay taxes.

As a dividend reinvestor, you should keep scrupulous records, including all statements, in order to determine the cost basis of shares when they are sold. The DRIP administrator will send you (and the IRS) a 1099-DIV form, usually by the end of February for the previous tax year. This form will show the taxable dividends paid, as well as any fees or commissions paid on your behalf. This record-keeping is crucial so you can calculate your total costs or cost basis for the investment. Without that calculation, you will end up paying more taxes.

When you sell an investment, you must pay tax on any capital gains. That's the difference between how much you paid for the stock and how much cash you got when you sold the stock. To minimize the capital gains taxes you pay, be sure you keep track of all your costs in buying that stock. We show you how to calculate capital gains later in the chapter.

When keeping records of costs, you need to consider everything you paid, as well as everything the DRIP or DSP company may have paid. Sometimes companies that sponsor DRIPs or DSPs pay fees and commissions on your behalf.

The IRS requires that the investor report any amount paid on your behalf by the DRIP or DSP company as extra taxable income. The amount paid will show up on the 1099-DIV form, as well as on account statements. However, any amount paid on your behalf in fees and commissions reduces the capital gains when a stock is sold.

Direct Aids

If you want help keeping track of your DRIPs, you may find the DRIP Wizard (www.dripwizard.com) a helpful software product for keeping records and calculating your tax bite.

If all this seems complicated—it is. A lifetime of DRIP investing may create a morass of tax obligations when the time comes to sell the DRIP shares. Each year you create at least four new cost bases of DRIP shares when dividends are reinvested. If you make additional cash investments, each one of those will have a new cost basis. It is likely that each time you purchase additional shares, whether through dividend reinvestments or additional cash investments, you will have a new cost basis.

Now that we've introduced the basics of DRIP and DSP taxation, let's take a closer look at the key DRIP and DSP transactions that will affect how you file your taxes. Some key things to consider include dividends, dividend reinvestments, commissions, fees, and purchase discounts.

Dividends

Whether you reinvest your dividends or not, they are considered a form of income. The amount should be included on the "dividends" line when you file your taxes with the IRS using Form 1040 or 1040A.

You should also report that amount on Schedule B of Form 1040 or Schedule 1 of Form 1040A. You should find the amount of total dividends on the 1099-DIV that you will get from each of your DRIP and DSP administrators. Add the total of all your dividends from all your 1099-DIV forms and put the total on the appropriate IRS forms.

Purchase Pitfalls

You must pay taxes on dividends even if you don't take the money as cash. Don't forget to report them when you file your taxes each year.

Dividend Reinvestment

Dividends you reinvest are still considered income. You must include the reinvested dividends in your total on Form 1040 or 1040A, as well as on Schedule B (Form 1040) or Schedule 1 (Form 1040A).

Commissions

Commissions, also known as brokerage fees, must be tracked even if your DRIP or DSP administrator pays commissions to buy your shares (which is common). You should include that information on the 1099-DIV form.

No matter who pays the commission—you or the company administrator—your cost basis of the shares being purchased or sold is increased. Be sure to keep careful records of any commissions paid. The records will help to decrease any capital gains you will have to pay when you sell your shares. We show you how to calculate capital gains later in the chapter.

Fees

If the DRIP or DSP company pays fees for you, they must be reported as dividend income. You will find a total of any fees paid on the 1099-DIV that you get from the DRIP or DSP administrator each year.

If you itemize your deductions, you can deduct any income you get based on fees as an investment expense. You list investment expenses on IRS Form 1040, Schedule A.

Purchase Discounts

Some companies provide you with a discounted purchase price when you buy stock. Any discount you get must be reported as dividend income in the year you get the discount.

For example, suppose a DRIP gives you a 5 percent discount on stock purchases. If you purchase $300 worth of stock, the discount would be $15 and you would get $315 worth of stock instead. You would need to report that extra $15 as dividend income. Purchase discounts will be reported on the 1099-DIV form that you get from the DRIP or DSP administrator each year.

Since DRIP and DSP tax reporting can be complicated, if you're not sure what to do with the forms when you get them from your DRIP or DSP administrator, check with your tax advisor. You certainly don't want to risk an IRS audit.

DRIP Tax Reporting Differences

Companies design their DRIPs with different features that can complicate your tax life even more.

Some DRIP administrators charge a periodic service charge, which gets deducted from your dividends. You'll get less stock to pay that fee. For example, a company may charge you $25 per year to administer your DRIP. Don't forget to keep track of those fees because they should be added to the cost basis of your stock.

Some DRIP administrators acquire stock directly from the company that is sponsoring the DRIP or DSP, while others buy shares on the stock market paying a brokerage firm a commission for handling the transaction. If your DRIP or DSP buys shares on the stock market there will be brokerage costs. You need to track those brokerage costs. Essentially, when the transaction is made you will get fewer shares of stock to cover those costs. For example, if your dividend reinvestment was $100 and the transaction fee for purchasing stock was $2, then you would only get $98 in stock purchases.

Some companies that maintain DRIPs will pay brokerage commission costs on purchases made through the plan. Others pay commissions out of the dividend and reduce the number of shares you receive. Be sure you know how your company pays the brokerage fees so you can accurately track your cost basis.

Some companies pay your commissions rather than deducting them from the dividend. Your share of the commission is treated as a dividend.

Some companies provide a discount on dividend reinvestment purchases—the amount of the discount is treated as an additional dividend. The same is true if you get a discount on additional purchases.

Before you sign up with a plan you should get a prospectus, in which there should be a discussion of the tax impacts of DRIP or DSP investing. The company should point out key tax issues and how you should deal with them. Show the prospectus to your tax advisor when you do your taxes. That way you can be sure you are reporting your DRIP and DSP transactions accurately.

Tax law treats you as the owner of the shares you hold in a DRIP or DSP even if the trustee or administrator holds the shares. For tax purposes your shares are not held in trust. The administrator of a DRIP or DSP is merely acting as your agent. This is the same role as a stockbroker would have, and you should treat the ownership of a DRIP or DSP in the same way as you would any stockholding with a broker.

If you decide to close your DRIP account and transfer the shares to a brokerage firm or hold them yourself in paper certificates, you do not have to report that as income. But if you sell the shares in your DRIP or DSP account you will have to report any capital gains you made on the sale.

Capital Gains Calculation

In order to calculate your capital gains, you will need certain information:

- The number of shares sold
- Selling price per share
- *Cost basis* per share

Calculating the cost basis will be your most difficult task. The official word from the tax code about how to determine cost basis states: "If you buy and sell

securities at different times in varying quantities
and you cannot definitely identify the securities
you sell, then figure the basis of those shares under
the first-in-first-out (FIFO) method—that is, the
first securities you acquired are the first sold."

def•i•ni•tion

> The **cost basis** is the dollar amount you
> paid for the stock. It will include the price
> of the stock plus any costs incurred, such
> as commissions, paid to buy the stock.

Currently the IRS sees DRIP purchases as not
identifiable, so the FIFO method is the one you
should use, unless your tax adviser recommends
something different.

Once you do know these three key items—number
of shares sold, selling price per share, and cost basis
per share—you calculate capital gains using this
formula:

Capital gains = number of shares sold ×
(selling price per share – cost basis of share)

Since your commissions and fees may differ with
each purchase, here's how you can find the average
cost basis per share for your stock.

To find the average cost basis, you would:

- List the cost of each share purchased that you are selling. For example, if you are selling 50 shares, then calculate the cost of the first 50 shares you bought. You may have a different cost basis for each share but luckily you don't have to calculate each share individually.

- Total the amount you spent on purchasing the first 50 shares, including the cost of the stock as well as any commission or fees you paid, and then divide that amount by 50.

- Use the average cost basis as the cost per share for calculating capital gains.

You may want to double check your calculations with your tax advisor to be sure you've done them correctly.

Tax Strategies

You may also decide to use other tax strategies, such as leaving stock to your heirs or simplifying your capital gains calculations.

Suppose you decide that you want to leave your stock to your grandchildren and never sell it while you are alive. If you never sold your DRIP stocks during your life, the DRIP shares would be left to your heirs as part of your estate.

The market value for all the shares will be stepped up to their value on the date of your death (or as of the date six months following your death). The decision on the timing for the stepped up price will be made by the person administering your estate. This eliminates the need to establish the historical cost basis of DRIP shares.

If you sell your DRIP or DSP shares, you can minimize the calculations by selling all the shares in a particular DRIP at the same time. This will create just two entries on your tax return, one for short-term capital gains from the dividends reinvested in the prior 12 months, and one for long-term capital gains (the sum of all the gains in the DRIP less the recent reinvestments).

When you calculate the average cost basis for your shares, you can total all cash investments plus all dividend reinvestments plus all fees plus all commissions you paid over the years. Then you divide that grand total by the number of shares you hold and you'll find an average cost basis for each share.

You can now understand the importance of record-keeping. Without it, you won't be able to prove the cost basis and you will end up paying high capital gains taxes. Unlike other tax-related documents, you should keep DRIP and DSP statements, recording all reinvestments and optional cash purchases (OCPs), until you sell your DRIP or DSP.

Once you sell the DRIP or DSP, you'll still need to hold on to your records for another three or four years. The IRS can audit your return anytime during the three years after you report the sale of the stock. Check with your tax advisor to find out how long he or she recommends you keep records of the DRIP or DSP transactions.

Yes, tax recordkeeping and calculations can be complicated, but being able to slowly build a long-term stock portfolio will be worth the extra effort you need to put into recordkeeping.

The Least You Need to Know

- You need to keep track of every penny you spend on your DRIPs and DSPs to prove your cost basis and minimize your capital gains tax.

- Not every DRIP or DSP company handles the costs of investing in the same way. Be sure you understand how the company you hold stock with handles commissions, fees, and discounts.

- Learn how to calculate capital gains and know what records you must keep in order to do that calculation.

- You can avoid having to calculate capital gains by leaving the shares to your heirs.

Glossary

account administrator Handles DSPs and DRIPs for companies. This is usually a bank that tracks stock and dividend reinvestments and maintains customer accounts.

ACH Automated Clearing House, a national network that facilitates electronic transfers between banks and other financial institutions.

aggregate To pull together transactions from a number of different DSP or DRIP account holders.

asset allocation The process of dividing investments among different kinds of assets—such as stocks, bonds, real estate, and cash—to minimize risk and meet your long-term goals.

capital gains Profits that come from selling shares at a higher price than the original cost.

cost basis The calculated cost of a particular share or group of shares of stock.

dollar-cost averaging An investment strategy where you invest equal dollar amounts regularly and periodically (such as $100 monthly) in a particular investment or portfolio. When you use this strategy, you purchase shares when prices are low and sell shares when prices are high. This strategy over the long term lowers the total average cost per share of the investment.

electronic funds transfer (EFT)   A method of moving cash from an account at one bank or institution to another.

exchange-traded funds (ETFs)   These track an index, but can be traded like a stock. They are a basket of stocks, just like a mutual fund, but they can be traded throughout the day while a mutual fund can only be traded at the end of the day based on its net asset value.

independent IRA custodians   Allow you to direct your retirement funds invested to any qualified investment that meets your investment requirements.

institutional investors   Large investors, which can include investment companies, mutual funds, insurance companies, pension funds, investment banks, or endowment funds. They make up the majority of shareholders in many companies.

Medallion Signature Guarantee   A formal program used by banks and other institutions to verify an individual's signature, usually required when transferring stock certificates.

no-load mutual funds   A portfolio of stocks managed by a professional stock manager, but you don't have to pay an up-front commission to buy the mutual fund's shares.

nondiscretionary trustee A trustee that has no discretion or personal decision-making power in your investment choices.

optional cash purchases (OCPs) Permitted by most companies that offer DRIPs. They enable you to buy shares in addition to your dividend reinvestment.

proxy record date The date of record on which owners are set by the company to determine who can vote at the annual or general meeting. You must own shares of stock on that date in order to vote on a company issue of concern to stockholders.

street name Means the stock is registered in the name of your brokerage firm on the issuer's books. Your brokerage firm holds the security for you in "book-entry" form. "Book-entry" simply means that you do not receive a certificate. Instead, your broker keeps a record in their books that you own that particular security.

synthetic DRIPs Not really DRIPs, but brokerage accounts with firms that allow you to reinvest your dividends at no cost. This is a service provided by some brokers.

tax lot A group of security holdings in an account usually purchased on the same date and used for tax reporting purposes.

transfer agent Hired by a corporation to maintain shareholder records, including purchases, sales, and account balances.

Resources

Following you will find websites and contact information for the best resources in direct stock investing.

Top Direct Stock Investing Websites

These are some of the best websites on which you can find general DRIP and DSP information.

DripCentral (www.dripcentral.com)

This website is managed by author Douglas Gerlach. He lists good choices in his online book about direct stock investing.

DRIP Wizard

If you want help keeping track of your DRIPs, you may find the DRIP Wizard (www.dripwizard.com) a helpful software product for keeping records and calculating your tax bite.

The Moneypaper

The Moneypaper (www.directinvesting.com) offers you a database of 1,300 companies that offer direct stock investing opportunities. You can also find excellent information about the basics of direct stock investing.

Wall-Street.com

Wall-Street.com (www.wall-street.com/directlist. html) focuses on about 700 companies that they believe have the most potential. They have confined their list to those companies that the American Association of Individual Investors covers for its members.

DRIP and DSP Account Administrators

You will actually open your DRIP or DSP with an account administrator rather than the company in most cases. Here is contact information for some of the top administrators.

Bank of New York Mellon

The Bank of New York Mellon (www.melloninvestor. com/isd) is the administrator for 547 companies that offer DRIP or DSP options. You can view plan summaries, plan material, and compare plans. If the company allows, you can even start your investment online. (That option does vary by company, as not every company allows online transactions.)

You can call them at 1-800-205-7699. You can also request a prospectus and application via e-mail at shrrelations@mellon.com or you can contact them by snail mail:

BNY/Mellon Shareowner Services
PO Box 358016
Pittsburgh, PA 15252

Registered or Overnight Mail:
BNY/Mellon Shareowner Services
480 Washington Boulevard
Jersey City, NJ 07310

Registrar and Transfer Company

The Registrar and Transfer Company is the transfer agent for over 150 companies that offer DRIP plans. You can research companies online at www.rtco.com/inv/drp.asp and download plan prospectuses and enrollment forms.

If you don't want to request information online, you can review the list of companies and call for information about the companies that interest you at 1-800-368-5948 or you can send snail mail to the investor relations department at:

Registrar and Transfer Company
ATTN: Investor Relations Department
10 Commerce Drive
Cranford, NJ 07016

Wells Fargo

Wells Fargo administers over 100 dividend reinvestment and direct purchase plans that you can research online at www.wellsfargo.com/com/shareowner_services/. You can also get plan material and enrollment forms by calling Shareowner Services at 1-800-401-1957. You can also contact Wells Fargo using snail mail at:

Shareowner Services
PO Box 64874
St Paul, MN 55164-0874

Those are three of the top account administrators. Other key account administrators include:

- American Stock Transfer (www.amstock.com)
- Computershare (www.computershare.com)
- Continental Stock Transfer (www.continentalstock.com)
- Corporate Stock Transfer (www.corporatestock.com)
- Interwest Transfer Co. (www.interwesttc.com)

Buying Your First Share

In order to open a DRIP, you have to buy at least one share of stock—and for some companies, more than one share. Here are some good sources for purchasing those first shares of stock.

Bank of New York Mellon

The Bank of New York Mellon's Investor Services Direct (https://vault.bnymellon.com/isd/) makes it easy for investors to buy their first share of stock plus additional shares of stock with the companies whose direct stock programs it administers. When you get to the website, click on Investment Plan Enrollment to search the available plans and download plan enrollment details for all the companies the bank handles. If you ask for an alphabetical list, you'll find a list of about 550 companies from which to choose.

Even if you don't plan to purchase through the Bank of New York Mellon, you'll find it much easier to get plan documents using its online research tool.

BetterInvesting

BetterInvesting, formerly NAIC (www.
betterinvesting.org), is a not-for-profit organization
of investment clubs and individual investors. They
offer investment education for both the novice and
experienced investors.

You can join BetterInvesting for $79 per year, which
includes a subscription to *BetterInvesting Magazine*.
By joining you will have access to the MyStockFund
stock purchase plan. This plan allows individuals to
one free stock purchase monthly for the first year of
their membership. You can contact BetterInvesting
with your membership questions by e-mail, telephone, or fax at:

E-mail: service@betterinvesting.org
Toll free: 1-877-275-6242
Telephone: 248-583-6242
Fax: 248-583-4880

First Share

First Share (www.firstshare.com) is a membership
organization that facilitates the purchase and sale of
an initial share of common stock for companies that
offer DRIPs. It matches a First Share member who
wishes to buy a stock in a particular company with a
member who is willing to sell a single share of stock
to another First Share member.

First Share maintains a database of members who own
shares in the companies qualified for the First Share
program and who have offered to sell single shares to
other members. When a member submits a request

to First Share to purchase one share of a company,
First Share refers the request to a member who is
willing to sell a share of the company requested.

ShareBuilder

ShareBuilder (www.sharebuilder.com) offers a full
range of services, including automatic investing that
allows you to buy stocks in whole dollar amounts.

Independent IRA Custodian Companies

If you want to invest in DRIPs or DSPs using an IRA,
you will need to open the account with an independent
IRA custodian. Here are three major independent IRA
custodian companies that you can use.

IRA Services

IRA Services (www.iraservices.com) has been provid-
ing retirement program services for over 30 years.
The company currently administers over 19,000
retirement accounts invested in a wide variety of
standard and nonstandard assets, including limited
partnerships, limited liability companies, promissory
notes (secured and unsecured), real estate investment
trusts, real estate land and income properties, private
placements, mutual funds, and stock in public and
private companies. You can call IRS Services at 650-
593-2221.

Pensco Trust Company

Pensco Trust Company's (www.penscotrust.com) sole business has been supporting self-directed IRAs since 1989. Pensco is chartered in New Hampshire and focuses on being the country's preferred special asset custodian for self-directed IRAs. You can call for more information about Pensco's services at 1-800-969-4472.

Sunwest Trust

Sunwest Trust (www.sunwesttrust.com) offers you the opportunity to self-direct your IRA in a wide variety of retirement plans, including Roth IRAs, spousal and traditional IRAs, SEPs, and SIMPLEs. Sunwest Trust acts as custodian for your retirement account while allowing you to direct the investments within your account. You can call Sunwest Trust for more information at 1-800-642-7167.

Appendix C

Top DRIP Companies

This list of top DRIP companies was developed using information in the database at www.directinvesting.com, administered by The Moneypaper, a leader in DRIP investing. You can find information about more than 1,300 companies that offer direct investment options at The Moneypaper website.

Abbott Laboratories (ABT)
Transfer agent: Computershare—1-800-332-2268

AFLAC Incorporated (AFL)
Transfer agent: AFLAC Inc.—1-800-235-2667

AGL Resources Inc. (AGL)
Transfer agent: Wells Fargo Bank—1-800-468-9716

Altria Group Inc. (MO)
Transfer agent: Computershare—1-800-442-0077

American Electric Power (AEP)
Transfer agent: Computershare—1-800-328-6955

American Express Co. (AXP)
Transfer agent: BNY/Mellon—1-800-463-5911

American Greetings Corp. A (AM)
Transfer agent: National City Bank—
1-800-622-6757

Anworth Mortgage Asset Corporation (ANH)
Transfer agent: American Stock Transfer—
1-877-248-6410

Archer-Daniels-Midland Company (ADM)
Transfer agent: Hickory Point Bank—1-888-740-5512

AstraZeneca Group plc (AZN)
Transfer agent: JPMorgan Chase Bank—
1-800-428-4237

AT&T Inc. (T)
Transfer agent: Computershare—1-800-351-7221

Avery Dennison Corp. (AVY)
Transfer agent: Computershare—1-800-756-8200

Avon Products Inc. (AVP)
Transfer agent: Computershare—781-575-2723

BancorpSouth Inc. (BXS)
Transfer agent: Registrar and Transfer Co.—
1-800-525-7686

Baxter International Inc. (BAX)
Transfer agent: Computershare—1-888-359-8645

Becton Dickinson and Co. (BDX)
Transfer agent: Computershare—1-800-955-4742

Boeing Co. (The) (BA)
Transfer agent: Computershare—1-888-777-0923

BP Plc (BP)
Transfer agent: JPMorgan Chase Bank—
1-877-638-5672

Bristol-Myers Squibb (BMY)
Transfer agent: BNY/Mellon—1-800-356-2026

Burlington Northern Santa Fe Corp. (BNI)
Transfer agent: Computershare—1-800-526-5678

Cabot Corporation (CBT)
Transfer agent: Computershare—781-575-3170

California Water Service Group (CWT)
Transfer agent: American Stock Transfer—
1-888-888-0316

Campbell Soup Co. (CPB)
Transfer agent: Computershare—1-800-446-2617

Caterpillar Inc. (CAT)
Transfer agent: BNY/Mellon—1-866-203-6622

Chemical Financial Corp. (CHFC)
Transfer agent: Computershare—1-800-942-5909

Chesapeake Utilities Corp. (CPK)
Transfer agent: Computershare—1-877-498-8865

Chevron Corp. (CVX)
Transfer agent: BNY/Mellon—1-800-368-8357

Citizens and Northern Corporation (CZNC)
Transfer agent: American Stock Transfer—
1-888-200-3166

Clorox Company (The) (CLX)
Transfer agent: Computershare—1-800-756-8200

Coca-Cola Co. (The) (KO)
Transfer agent: Computershare—1-888-265-3747

Colgate-Palmolive Company (CL)
Transfer agent: BNY/Mellon—1-800-756-8700

ConAgra Foods Inc. (CAG)
Transfer agent: Wells Fargo Bank—1-800-214-0349

Conoco Phillips (COP)
Transfer agent: BNY/Mellon—1-800-356-0066

Consolidated Edison Inc. (ED)
Transfer agent: BNY/Mellon—1-800-522-5522

Cracker Barrel Old Country Store Inc. (CBRL)
Transfer agent: American Stock Transfer—
1-800-485-1883

Deere and Company (DE)
Transfer agent: BNY/Mellon—1-800-268-7369

Diebold Inc. (DBD)
Transfer agent: BNY/Mellon—1-866-242-7752

Dow Chemical (DOW)
Transfer agent: BNY/Mellon—1-800-369-5606

DTE Energy Co. (DTE)
Transfer agent: BNY/Mellon—1-866-388-8558

DuPont (E.I.) (DD)
Transfer agent: Computershare—1-888-983-8766

Ecolab Inc. (ECL)
Transfer agent: Computershare—1-800-322-8325

Edison International (EIX)
Transfer agent: Wells Fargo Bank—1-800-347-8625

Entergy Corp. (ETR)
Transfer agent: BNY/Mellon—1-800-333-4368

Equity Residential Property Trust (EQR)
Transfer agent: Computershare—1-800-733-5001

Exelon Corporation (EXC)
Transfer agent: BNY/Mellon—1-800-626-8729

Exxon Mobil Corp. (XOM)
Transfer agent: Computershare—1-800-252-1800

Federal Realty Investment Trust (FRT)
Transfer agent: American Stock Transfer—
1-800-937-5449

GATX Corp. (GMT)
Transfer agent: BNY/Mellon—1-800-851-9677

GlaxoSmithKline plc (GSK)
Transfer agent: BNY/Mellon—1-888-269-2377

Goodrich Corporation (GR)
Transfer agent: BNY/Mellon—1-866-557-8700

H.J. Heinz Company (HNZ)
Transfer agent: Wells Fargo Bank—651-450-4064

Hancock Holding Co. (HBHC)
Transfer agent: Hancock Bank Corporate Trust
Dept.—228-563-7657

Harris Corp. (HRS)
Transfer agent: BNY/Mellon—1-888-261-6777

Hasbro Inc. (HAS)
Transfer agent: Computershare—1-800-733-5001

Health Care REIT (HCN)
Transfer agent: BNY/Mellon—1-888-216-7206

Healthcare Realty Trust (HR)
Transfer agent: Computershare—781-575-3400

Hershey Company (The) (HSY)
Transfer agent: BNY/Mellon—1-800-851-4216

Home Depot (The) Inc. (HD)
Transfer agent: Computershare—1-800-577-0177

Hormel Foods Corp. (HRL)
Transfer agent: Wells Fargo Bank—1-877-536-3559

Illinois Tool Works Inc. (ITW)
Transfer agent: Computershare—1-888-829-7424

Ingersoll-Rand (IR)
Transfer agent: BNY/Mellon—1-866-229-8405

International Business Machines (IBM)
Transfer agent: Computershare—1-888-426-6700

ITT Corp. (ITT)
Transfer agent: BNY/Mellon—1-800-254-2823

J.C. Penney Company Inc. (JCP)
Transfer agent: BNY/Mellon—1-800-842-9470

Johnson & Johnson (JNJ)
Transfer agent: Computershare—1-800-328-9033

Johnson Controls Inc. (JCI)
Transfer agent: Wells Fargo Bank—1-877-602-7397

Kellogg Company (K)
Transfer agent: Wells Fargo Bank—1-877-910-5385

Kimberly-Clark Corp. (KMB)
Transfer agent: Computershare—1-800-730-4001

Kraft Foods Inc. (KFT)
Transfer agent: Wells Fargo Bank—1-866-655-7238

Lancaster Colony Corp. (LANC)
Transfer agent: American Stock Transfer—
1-800-937-5449

Liberty Property Trust (LRY)
Transfer agent: Wells Fargo Bank—1-800-944-2214

Lockheed Martin Corporation (LMT)
Transfer agent: Computershare—1-877-498-8861

Louisiana-Pacific Corporation (LPX)
Transfer agent: Computershare—781-575-2726

McDonald's Corp. (MCD)
Transfer agent: Computershare—1-800-621-7625

Medtronic Inc. (MDT)
Transfer agent: Wells Fargo Bank—1-888-648-8154

Merck and Company Inc. (MRK)
Transfer agent: Wells Fargo Bank—1-888-291-3713

Microsoft Corporation (MSFT)
Transfer agent: American Stock Transfer—
1-800-285-7772

Morgan Stanley (MS)
Transfer agent: BNY/Mellon—1-800-622-2393

National Fuel Gas Company (NFG)
Transfer agent: BNY/Mellon—1-800-648-8166

National Retail Properties Inc. (NNN)
Transfer agent: American Stock Transfer—
1-800-937-5449

Nationwide Health Properties Inc. (NHP)
Transfer agent: BNY/Mellon—1-800-524-4458

New Jersey Resources Corp. (NJR)
Transfer agent: Computershare—1-800-817-3955

Nike Inc. (NKE)
Transfer agent: Computershare—1-800-756-8200

Norfolk Southern Corp. (NSC)
Transfer agent: BNY/Mellon—212-815-4087

Northrop Grumman Corp. (NOC)
Transfer agent: Computershare—1-800-756-8200

Northwest Natural Gas Co. (NWN)
Transfer agent: American Stock Transfer—
1-888-777-0321

Novartis AG (NVS)
Transfer agent: JPMorgan Chase Bank—
1-877-816-5333

Nucor Corp. (NUE)
Transfer agent: American Stock Transfer—
1-800-937-5449

Occidental Petroleum Corp. (OXY)
Transfer agent: BNY/Mellon—1-800-622-9231

Paychex Inc. (PAYX)
Transfer agent: American Stock Transfer—
1-877-814-9688

PepsiCo Inc. (PEP)
Transfer agent: BNY/Mellon—1-800-226-0083

Pfizer Inc. (PFE)
Transfer agent: Computershare—1-800-733-9393

PG&E Corp. (PCG)
Transfer agent: BNY/Mellon—1-800-719-9056

Philip Morris International (PM)
Transfer agent: Computershare—1-877-745-935

Piedmont Natural Gas Company (PNY)
Transfer agent: American Stock Transfer—
1-800-937-5449

Pitney Bowes Inc. (PBI)
Transfer agent: Computershare—1-800-648-8170

Polaris Industries Inc. (PII)
Transfer agent: Wells Fargo Bank—1-800-468-9716

Procter and Gamble Co. (PG)
Transfer agent: Procter and Gamble Co.—
1-800-742-6253

Progress Energy Inc. (PGN)
Transfer agent: Computershare—1-866-290-4388

Quaker Chemical Corp. (KWR)
Transfer agent: American Stock Transfer—
1-800-278-4353

Raytheon Company (RTN)
Transfer agent: American Stock Transfer—
1-800-360-4519

Reynolds American Inc. (RAI)
Transfer agent: BNY/Mellon—1-877-679-5701

Royal Dutch Shell Class A (RDS.A)
Transfer agent: BNY/Mellon—1-888-269-2377

Sanofi-Aventis (SNY)
Transfer agent: JPMorgan Chase Bank—
1-877-272-9475

SCANA Corp. (SCG)
Transfer agent: SCANA Corp.—1-800-763-5891

Sempra Energy (SRE)
Transfer agent: American Stock Transfer—
1-877-773-6772

Simon Property Group (SPG)
Transfer agent: BNY/Mellon—1-800-454-9768

Snap-on Incorporated (SNA)
Transfer agent: Computershare—1-800-446-2617

Tanger Factory Outlet Centers Inc. (SKT)
Transfer agent: Computershare—781-575-3170

Travelers Companies Inc. (The) (TRV)
Transfer agent: Wells Fargo Bank—1-888-326-5102

Union Pacific Corp. (UNP)
Transfer agent: Computershare—1-800-317-2512

United Parcel Service Inc. (UPS)
Transfer agent: BNY/Mellon—1-800-758-4674

United Technologies (UTX)
Transfer agent: Computershare—1-800-488-9281

Valley National Bancorp (VLY)
Transfer agent: American Stock Transfer—
1-800-278-4353

Verizon Communications Inc. (VZ)
Transfer agent: Computershare—1-800-631-2355

Wal-Mart Stores Inc. (WMT)
Transfer agent: Computershare—1-800-438-6278

Waste Management Inc. (WMI)
Transfer agent: BNY/Mellon—1-800-969-1190

Wells Fargo and Company (WFC)
Transfer agent: Wells Fargo Bank—1-877-840-0492

Whirlpool Corp. (WHR)
Transfer agent: Computershare—1-800-446-2617

Xcel Energy Inc. (XEL)
Transfer agent: Wells Fargo Bank—651-450-4064

XTO Energy Inc. (XTO)
Transfer agent: BNY/Mellon—1-888-877-2892

Index

F

E